FOREWORD BY PASTOR HENRY MADAVA

Bound Together by Pain

KARY ROWEN

Baruch

Unless otherwise identified,
Scripture quotations are from
the New International Version of the Bible.

Baruch Publishing
www.baruch-books.com

BOUND TOGETHER BY PAIN
by Kary Rowen

ISBN

For Worldwide Distribution

Publishing books, ebooks and audio books
in different languages,
Email: **office@baruch-books.com**

Contents

Acknowledgement

Writing a book is not as easy as it seems at first glance. But when God puts a burden on your heart, you can't resist. At one point I realized that I had no right to refuse sharing what had helped me and many women obtain freedom from many troubles. Therefore, first of all, I thank the Lord for putting this book on my heart.

———◆———

Thank you Pastor Henry, for showing us the meaning of life and for the teachings that liberate and bring life to those who have already given up and lost hope. Thank you for agreeing to do this difficult work of helping to change the lives of people, as well as to bring freedom and healing. Thank you for the social project, "Ukraine Without Drugs". Thank you for many rehabilitation centers and outpatient programs. Thank you for the price you pay, for believing in and supporting us, and for your contribution to my life.

———◆———

Thank you Yaroslav, that you often sacrificed your rest and interests to support me in the process of writing this book. This book is the fruit of our joint efforts. It was birthed, like a child. All the time I was carrying it, you were close by. Maybe we will birth another book which will reveal the other side of the problem.

Thank you to my spouse. You are the best husband in the world!

———·◆·———

I thank everyone who helped me: Serhei Anatolievich Dovzhenko, Maia Serheievna Oprishko, Elena Ivanovna Kopeichenko, Viktoriia Pohoskaia and many others. Thank you for serving with all your heart.

———·◆·———

Thank you that you believed in God and trusted me to help you solve your problems. Thank you that you let me touch your lives and serve you! It is a great honor to be a tool in God's hands and see how He changes the lives of people.

 Karina Yarovenko

Endorsements

This was an unforgettable time for me. God gave my wife the desire to write a book that would describe our experience of serving addicts and their families and running into some of the same difficulties each time.

I am the only person who has watched the whole process of writing this book and have walked through the real stories of many of the people set out here.

This book was written on land, water and in the air. I listened to new chapters being written in many countries: Ukraine, Russia, Thailand and the United Arab Emirates. We discussed the principles which were given by God exactly for the specific situations of those people to whom we served at home, at work and on mission trips.

I'm glad that Karina has written her first book, and it won't be the last one! It will help many people deal with the problem of addiction and understand its core and nature. If you know the enemy, it is easier to fight and win with God's help.

ℭ Yaroslav Yarovenko

————— •◆• —————

Having read this book, the only thing I regret is that it didn't fall into my hands at that most difficult time, when I, like the heroines written about here, was trying to understand why everything had happened to me. I am grateful to the author for not only describing the lives of women whose husbands have been addicted, but most importantly, for showing the way out.

∾ Inna Yarovenko

Even if there are no such problems in your family, read this book anyway! It will inspire you to believe in victory even in the most hopeless situation, and help you to hold onto God and hasten this victory with your thoughts and deeds.

∾ Svetlana Merhasova

Foreword

T he book "Bound Together by Pain" is a profound, skillful and unique description of a very real and painful problem of today's society. It is not difficult to find oneself in the characters of this book. It is not only for those whose spouses or parents are addicted, but also for those who are the addicts! This book is unique due to the fact that it contains deep and effective principles of how to escape from such a binding web! This book can be used in working with the distressed and reads like an intriguing novel! I recommend everyone to read and enjoy this unique work!

It was my dream that someone would write a book like this, based on their own experience. Karina did an exceptional job in fulfilling this dream!

 Pastor Henry Madava

Introduction

This book was written not by a doctor of psychology, a narcologist or by another expert, of which there are many. I in no way diminish the significance of the work of these professionals and I thank them for the job they do. But I really wanted to publish a book based on real life stories of people whose lives were changed not because of science, which states that there are no "former drug addicts" (and alcoholics), but because of the knowledge of the truth that sets people free forever.

I want to share with you what can change your entire life and the lives of people close to you. I want to share simple truths that can save a life and set them free from addiction. I want you to forget about the pain, fear and oppression. I want you to finally start living.

Dear readers, you may ask, "Where does this boldness come from? Who gave you the right to make such statements?" And I respond, "I walked through this horror and experienced that pain and fear. I'm one of those people who were desperately looking for a way out. I'm one who didn't know the purpose of life and had no desire to live. I'm one who doesn't speak from assumptions and speculations, but from real life experiences, from people saved by the Lord."

And now let me ask you a question: Do you want to be free from pain, fear, oppression, shame and hopelessness? If your answer is yes, I invite you to set off down the road. It will not be easy, but the reward for your efforts will be great. You will receive the valuable reward of life.

CHAPTER 1

Where Did the Trouble Come From?

It was a quiet summer evening. The smell of jasmine and lilac filled the air. It was daylight. Young women were traveling to a meeting from different parts of the city. Lorena, the director of a large manufacturing company, was going to be attending a meeting for the first time today. She was stuck in a traffic jam and couldn't break out of it. The whole Moscow Bridge was jammed up.

In the meantime, the meeting had already begun. Young, beautiful women had gathered. They were all married. Many of them had children. But they were not rushing home. They had come here. What had united them? Pain- the unbearable pain of an unhealthy marriage. This was a meeting of wives whose husbands were addicted, and it didn't matter to what- be it alcohol, drugs, gambling or some other misfortune, because there is so much evil today.

Finally Lorena got out of the traffic jam, and, having arrived at the place, literally flew into the room.

"Is this a fellowship group for codependents? I need to send my husband to a rehabilitation center or put him in the hospital," she said very quickly and confidently.

"Yes, good evening! You're in the right place. Please come in. We are going to drink tea and get acquainted," a young woman answered politely.

"It must be a psychologist," Lorena thought.

She didn't resist, went into the room and sat on a vacant chair. There were eight people in the room, and Lorena was surprised that all of them were happy.

"Tea, coffee? What would you like to drink?" Alla asked. She was responsible for food at the fellowship group.

"Nothing. I need your help. A friend advised me to contact you," stated Lorena. "Her husband was a drug addict, and many times I had told her to get a divorce, but she didn't dare. Some time ago I met her with her husband and didn't recognize him. He looked much better, and had gotten a job. He said he'd been in a rehabilitation center and had become drug free. He had even quitted smoking. So I need you to send my husband to a rehabilitation center."

"I understand, but what's your name?"

"Lorena."

"Nice to meet you. I'm Rita. And this is Alla." Rita introduced all the women to Lorena. "Lorena, a person goes to a rehabilitation center voluntarily. It must be their decision. We can't force them to go there," said Rita, the leader of the fellowship group.

"I knew you wouldn't help me. Once again I've believed in a fairy tale," Lorena answered shortly and with displeasure.

"You don't have to draw these kinds of conclusions. Let's get acquainted and talk. We will tell you about ourselves. Many of our husbands are already free.

And then, if you wish, you will tell what is happening to you."

"Well, since I'm already here, let's talk," Lorena answered.

"That's great. Dear Alla, can you tell your story to our guest?"

Before Alla could open her mouth, Vera flew into the room.

"Hi girls. Sorry, I'm late. Imagine, I took the wrong shuttle bus! Oh, sorry, the group has already started and I'm chatting. Can you believe, in front of the building a Porsche is parked and there's no way through! Probably its driver has just bought his driving license," Vera blurted out without stopping.

"That's my car," Lorena said, "and I didn't buy my license. There was no other place to park. They can't possibly improve the situation with parking in this city," Lorena complained.

"I'm sorry! I didn't mean to say anything bad. It's just that we usually don't park here like that."

"Okay, Vera, take a seat please. We didn't come here to discuss buses and parking, right?" The group leader said. "My dear, everyone's here, so let's begin. Well, Alla, go on." Everybody giggled and Rita too, because Alla didn't even have time to open her mouth. "Or rather, start telling your story," the leader continued.

"Well, if you please, I'm going to start from the very beginning, because the girls have never heard my full story, and now it's time to share it:

As a child, I was a normal girl and grew up in a normal family, like a lot of people. Seemingly, a normal child with a normal situation in a family. But it was only seemingly so. If I try to describe my childhood in a few words, the words would be: drinking... scandals... pause... and then all over again.

About my childhood, I remember that I knew for sure whether my father was drunk or sober only by the way he turned the key in the lock. It is unexplainable, but as a little girl, I knew the condition of my father before he would come into the apartment. I could even tell his level of intoxication by the sounds he made and the time he spent by the door. I was always afraid of this key turn, because I didn't know what to expect next. He often beat up my mom. He was violent to her. He didn't control his anger. He could beat her head against the wall, and when she fell, he kicked her. I was always afraid that someday he would kill her. And then so it happened: my father beat my mother to such an extent that she had to go to the hospital and soon died. But he wasn't put behind bars. You know, this kind of life is terrible because you love and hate your father simultaneously. There was a time when he was my hero and defender, and at the same time he was the person who killed my mother and became my vicious enemy.

A father is a defender. I remember how at school we all used to say, 'I'll tell my dad.' Every child believes that his father is able to solve all their problems. If only fathers understood what their children felt when they drank! Children become defenseless, and anyone can offend them.

Since my childhood I have learned to behave in a way so that no one could understand my feelings. God forbid that I would show I was unhappy with the fact that my father was a drunk. He controlled everyone by his behavior and mood. If he was in a good mood, everyone was fine. If his mood was bad, everyone wasn't doing well.

One minute I was dreaming that he would go somewhere or disappear completely, but the next time, I couldn't imagine my life without him. After all, he was the only family in my life.

Pain, resentment, hatred and fear filled my heart. When he slept at public transport stops or near stalls or found himself with the police, I was ashamed.

When you grow up in such a family, your soul is constantly overcome by fear, shame, hopelessness and pain.

You just want to scream to dads of all countries and continents to get out of alcoholism and drug addiction, because your children suffer!

So I lived, studied, spent time with friends, dreamt about the future, and at the same time there was a pain in my soul.

I grew up and began to secretly smoke, drink and take drugs. There wasn't a day that I didn't drink beer or vodka with my friends. In general, all these things lifted my spirits. I liked company and hung out every day. Afterward, my friends from one of these groups all died from a drug overdose. Because I hated my father, I decided to get married and run away. But I definitely knew that I didn't want to marry an alcoholic. Nevertheless, I got what I was afraid of. But it took some time before I knew that my husband was addicted. It only came out a few years after we had already had two children. My husband's drug addiction was a death sentence for me."

Lorena interrupted Alla and asked,

"I'm sorry that all this happened to you. Well, your dad drank and then you married an addict. According to psychology it all checks out. Subconsciously you were looking for such a person. I've read about this. But explain why it happened to me? Why did I get sucked in like that? Neither my father, nor my mother drank, fight or quarreled. If there were quarrels, they were petty!"

"Lorena, I'm glad you've brought this up. Indeed, it often happens that women whose parents drank and controlled other family members marry addicts, but it's not always the case. I'm going to try to answer you, and to do this, let's read the Bible, the wisest book," Rita replied.

"Why the Bible? What has that got to do with it?" Lorena asked.

"Dear Alla, thank you for sharing a part of your story. Next time, you can tell it to the very end: about your husband and your relationship with your father. And now I'm going to answer Lorena's question."

"Okay, I've already told you a lot, unlike the first attempt," Alla replied with a smile.

"Lorena, our classes are based on the Holy Scriptures, the Bible. And there are reasons for that. Just take your time and listen, and I'm going to get straight to the point."

Why are the classes based on the Bible?

Rita continued, "Many people listen to the advice of herbalists, healers, sages and various gurus. Those, who can afford it, go to India and look for a teacher. Some people visit fortune-tellers, psychics, hypnotists or read horoscopes. In the past, people have always looked for a way out, and they are still doing it today. People go to psychologists and psychotherapists who diagnose them, but in fact, we don't need just a diagnosis — we all want to find an answer. Some people turn to a higher intelligence, the cosmos, the universe, or nature. In such a way, people who haven't been able to solve their problems with the help of natural things appeal to the supernatural. But we have the opportunity to appeal to the living God. Only the One Who has created man, our Lord God, can show us the way out. Drug addiction, alcoholism and any other addiction are not just bad habits, but pain in the soul and are spiritual problems. God created the soul of man, and He as the Creator knows better how to fix it. In order to understand how God proposes to solve the problem of addiction, we need to know what He says. The Holy Scriptures are not just stories and words, but they are living truths which have real power. These words, if applied in our lives, can change everything- absolutely everything. Many of us present can testify to this."

"And where was God, when my husband began to use drugs? Where is He now, when I've been crying at nights for years? Why doesn't He help me?" Lorena asked.

"God was always with you, and He never left you. And today He is waiting for you to let Him deal with your problems. You are here now (and you, dear readers, are reading this book now) because God is not indifferent to your life and He wants to help you. If you agree, let's continue," Rita concluded.

"Okay, I agree," Lorena said. "I just want to understand where this problem came from. It's good that we will learn from the Bible. I would like to know everything in more detail. I agree that the Bible is a wise book. Does the Bible say something about why my husband started to take drugs? Why can nothing stop him? Why should my child suffer because of such a father?" Lorena asked.

"Well, Lorena, if the others don't mind, I'm going to answer your question," the leader said.

"I'm curious too," Vera said. "I just can't understand why this happens. Why do I have such a problem and why did it happen to me? How could I get sucked in like that? How can I get out of this place and where is the exit?"

"All right," Rita said. "Well, let's deal with this. It's really great of you all to decide to understand this. Often wives only say,

'Do something about him! Send him to a rehabilitation center! Just don't let him take drugs! Just don't let him drink!' It's like trying to make apples disappear from an apple tree without dealing with the tree roots. If we don't deal with the tree roots, the apples will grow again. It's only a matter of time.

When people try to deal with a problem, they usually start from childhood and traumas which could be the reasons why bad things happened in a normal family. Some of them go deeper and analyze the lives of the father and mother, grandfather and grandmother, if there is a history of addiction in the family. That's the right place to start, and Alla's case proves this. But to fully understand the cause of the problem, we need to go even deeper, to the very beginning.

So, let's open the Bible to the very beginning, the book of Genesis. The book of Genesis reveals to us how the earth and people were created, that is, how everything came into being. I hope, girls, that nobody here believes that we came from monkeys!"

The girls giggled. No one considered themselves a descendant of a monkey.

> Then God said, "Let Us make man in Our image, according to Our likeness; let them have dominion over the fish of the sea, over the birds of the air, and over the cattle, over all the earth and over every creeping thing that creeps on the earth." So God created man in His own image; in the image of God He created him; male and female He created them. Then God blessed them, and God said to them, "Be fruitful and multiply; fill the earth and subdue it; have dominion over the fish of the sea, over the birds of the air, and over every living thing that moves on the earth."
>
> ☙ Genesis 1:26–28

When God created Adam and Eve, He gave them dominion over the earth and all living beings on the earth. And also He gave them the task to tend and keep the garden. So, Adam and Eve had a full abundance of everything, as well as full power to use of all the resources on the earth. The only forbidden thing was eating the fruit of the tree of the knowledge of good and evil. Why did the Lord forbid them to do this? Because the fruit of this tree was deadly. God warned that as soon as they ate the fruit of this tree, they would have problems and die.

> Then the Lord God took the man and put him in the garden of Eden to tend and keep it. And the Lord God commanded the man, saying, "Of every tree of the garden you may freely eat; but of the tree of the knowledge of good and evil you shall not eat, for in the day that you eat of it you shall surely die."   ✎ Genesis 2:15–17

It is so like drugs. Everyone knows that drugs are dangerous, everyone knows about the consequences of alcohol, and everyone knows how it can end up. We were told about this. Parents often warn children about the danger of drugs, alcohol and other bad things. But children are often disobedient.

Despite God's warning, the people violated His commandment and were not serious and responsible about heeding His advice.

When the people violated the commandment of God, it seemed that they didn't do anything wrong. They just ate the fruit of the tree. They didn't kill anyone! But that was just at first glance. God warned them that they couldn't do that and that disobedience would cause death. Adam and Eve violated the commandment of God and because of that, they had problems. This must be repeated once more: **When a person violates the commandment of God, problems arise and eventually death comes.**

Look what is written in the book of Psalms:

> Those who sat in darkness and in the shadow of death, bound in affliction and irons — because they rebelled against the words of God.
> ✎ Psalm 107:10

Why did they sit in darkness? Why were they bound in affliction? Why were they enslaved? The Bible gives the answer. They rebelled against the words of God. They were disobedient to the commandments of God and lived according to their own desires, not according to the will of God. For those people, their own will was more important than the will of God. They didn't have an understanding of the authority of the words of God, and therefore they didn't obey His words.

The words of God lead to freedom, joy and life. Therefore, when a person doesn't obey His words, they get into trouble.

Girls, let me describe the way I see it. For example, my dad says to me, 'Daughter, you can't put a nail in the electric socket, because you will get an electric shock.' I don't listen to his words and do it anyway because I decide to try and see what is going to happen.

So, my father's words don't mean anything to me. I put a nail in the socket, when my dad isn't looking. I get an electric shock and die.

It is important to understand that God doesn't cause problems or kill people. He never plans evil events. God gave life to man, but death is caused by sin. God gives life. Think how many times we've broken the commandments God gave to people? Perhaps you didn't kill anyone in your life, but that doesn't mean that you didn't violate the law of God. In the book of Romans it says:

> For all have sinned and fall short of the glory of God... There is none righteous, no, not one.
>
> ✺ Romans 3:23, 10

I understand that compared to their husbands who are addicted to drugs or alcohol, the wives may think that they are angels on the earth. But this is not true. There is not a single person on earth who is completely righteous before God, because all have sinned.

Of course, it also happens that sometimes a person doesn't know what they've done wrong. But even according to the law written by people, ignorance of the law is no excuse. So why do we consider that ignorance of God's law can release us from responsibility and problems? The Bible says, 'My people are destroyed for lack of knowledge.' God doesn't want people to be destroyed, but for lack of knowledge of how to live, people still perish. If you break the traffic rules, there's a good chance that an accident will happen. If you violate the laws of the country, there's a good chance you'll go to jail. The world is created according to certain rules which operate regardless of whether or not a person knows them, and whether or not a person is a believer. If a person jumps out of a window from the twelfth floor, they will certainly fall down, and it will happen regardless of whether or not they believe in it or not, and whether or not they know about the law of gravity. It is the same thing in the spiritual world. If you break spiritual laws, problems arise. The law is not written in order to accuse someone, but in order to protect them from evil.

Breaking the commandment of God is a sin.

> So when the woman saw that the tree was good for food, that it was pleasant to the eyes, and a

tree desirable to make one wise, she took of its fruit and ate. She also gave to her husband with her, and he ate.   ᴄᴏ Genesis 3:6

This is how they violated the commandment of God, and through Adam, the first man, sin, as well as problems and illnesses, entered the lives of mankind. In such a way the power which God gave to people, was transferred from man to Satan! People themselves gave their power to Satan. By their disobedience they brought death into effect, and launched a system that destroys the earth and humanity."

For the wages of sin is death...
                    ᴄᴏ Romans 6:23

"Rita, I'm starting to get the idea. Tell me, is there any way out of this?" Lorena asked.

"Yes, Lorena, there is. Because of the fact that sin came into being, blood had to be shed. The Lord loves people, but sin can be washed away only by blood. Therefore, the blood of an absolutely innocent animal was shed to cleanse the guilty man.

But sin began to multiply more and more. Man needed a way out of that swamp, because he couldn't deal with sin. Cleansing with the blood of animals was a temporary solution, because man sins daily, often without even realizing it.

Then the Lord Himself came to the earth to save humanity.

For God so loved the world that He gave His only begotten Son, that whoever believes in Him should not perish but have everlasting life.

> For God didn't send His Son into the world to condemn the world, but that the world through Him might be saved. "He who believes in Him is not condemned; but he who does not believe is condemned already, because he has not believed in the name of the only begotten Son of God.   ∽ John 3:16-18

The Son of God, Jesus Christ, came to the earth in the form of a man. Jesus was sinless, and He shed His blood. The blood of an innocent man, the only sinless person, was shed, just like the blood of an innocent animal before. And His blood washed sin away.

Jesus was nailed to a cross. He died, but rose again on the third day. Thus, He gives salvation to all who believe in Him.

The Bible says:

> That if you confess with your mouth the Lord Jesus and believe in your heart that God has raised Him from the dead, you will be saved. For with the heart one believes unto righteousness, and with the mouth confession is made unto salvation.   ∽ Romans 10:9–10

It's very simple. If you believe in your heart that Jesus died for your sins and rose again on the third day for your justification, this will lead you to righteousness. But to be saved, you need to say this out loud, that is, to declare that He is your Lord.

Lorena, I suggest you take the first step — to be reconciled to God, to allow Him to cleanse you from sin and restore to you the power that was originally yours.

Do you believe that Jesus died for you and rose again for your justification?"

"Rita, I believe and understand that I've sinned a lot in my life," Lorena answered.

"Well, I'm going to lead you in prayer. Repeat this prayer aloud after me, so that you can hear it:

> Dear God,
>
> I realize that I am a sinner, and I ask You to forgive my sins and cleanse me from all unrighteousness. I believe that Jesus Christ, the Son of God, died for my sins and rose again on the third day for my justification. I ask You, Jesus, to come into my heart and to be my Lord and Savior from this day forward. I ask You to change me and my life, as well as completely lead my life and protect me from all evil. Change my life. Thank you that You hear and forgive me. Amen.

Lorena cried, but they were tears of joy. She reconciled with the Creator of Heaven and Earth, with the One who created and loved her. The woman said that prayer with all her heart. God forgave her, and she became His child.

"Lorena, now you have access to the Father. He hears your prayers and will answer them," continued Rita. "Sin separated you from God. Maybe you prayed before, but didn't get an answer. Now, that you are reconciled with Him through the sacrifice of Jesus Christ, you have direct access to God. Come to the Lord at any time and communicate with Him in your own words. He is alive. He hears you and will answer. This is the most important decision in your life- the most important choice! I congratulate you on this victory!"

Dear reader, we can't solve our problems without Jesus. If you missed the prayer of repentance, go back and pray to God. It is useless to fight the problem of addiction on your own. You need Jesus.

After the group, the girls drank tea and got to know each other better. Then they went outside.

"Look, I feel much better and feel relieved. Can you smell that fragrance? It's lilac! It's so peaceful and light. It's been a long time since I felt like that. And this warm and light breeze! I've been caught up in my own problems, but life is beautiful. I want to enjoy it again," Lorena said. For the first time she didn't run away at breakneck speed.

"Yes, Lorena, you're right. God made everything beautiful and gave us so many things to enjoy, but we forget to do this. We fuss, get angry and grumble. We don't have time to enjoy our children, their quirks and smiles. We are so consumed by our pain and bustle that we don't see and hear many things," Rita said.

"Thank you. I feel so rested after speaking with you. I will attend the group meetings," Lorena stated.

"Of course, please come," stated Rita.

"I can give somebody a lift. I'm going to Darnitsa," Lorena said.

"Me too. I'm with you," Vera responded.

Everyone went home.

Lorena parked her car in the parking lot and happily went home. In her soul there was hope that everything could be changed, that her son could have a good father and she could have a good husband, and that it would be possible to live without lies, drugs, quarrels and fights. How she wanted to believe in all of this!

She went into the apartment and felt sad again. Nothing had changed at home. Her husband had the same dead eyes which expressed nothing. It was just so sad....

For the next week, Lorena doubted whether or not to attend the group meeting. It felt a little strange and the problem with her husband was not resolved. Of course, she felt a little relieved, but how would that change the problem? It was so difficult to decide what to do next. But one thing was clear: something needed to be done.

CHAPTER 2

If He Has the Problems, Why Should I Change?

Lorena spent a week doubting and meditating, but finally decided to attend the group again. "The girls understand me. They've also gone through the same problem," she thought.

This time Lorena came in first, and she managed to talk to Rita privately.

"Rita, tell me what to do next. Maybe I should send him somewhere or even get a divorce. I'm so tired of it all. What should I do? Where do I need to start?"

"Well, Lorena, you asked an honest question. Here is an honest answer, okay?"

"Okay, Rita. I will try to understand."

"First, let me tell you about a phone call that got me thinking.

Being tired of the constant duty to 'love' my husband and help him, I was already exhausted and weak. Dark circles under my eyes, unhealthy thinness and a green complexion had become a constant part of my appearance. I was unwilling to put on make-up and update my wardrobe. I had no desire to cook, clean up, or to do anything else. Total apathy was so usual for me. Depression, stress, lack of sleep and oppression were my constant companions and friends.

When my husband and I visited some doctors, I was often offered to sit in the patient's chair, because many doctors didn't understand which of us was addicted.

Due to that state, I'd acquired problems with my immune system and was often sick.

I just couldn't save that person anymore, because I didn't have the energy.

On all sides, there were many advisors telling me what to do, how to love unconditionally and all that sort of thing, but I had no strength to do it.

Therefore, when my husband asked me to make a phone call to talk to another minister who started working with him, to put it mildly, I wasn't particularly enthused.

When I picked up the phone, I immediately began to say that I didn't have any strength and that I could no longer participate in saving my husband.

And what he actually said to me was, 'Take care of yourself!'

I thought, 'What? Why?' I was so confused. I couldn't understand that shocking phrase. What did it mean to take care of myself? In what sense?

Then I thought, 'Well, first of all, change your hair and buy new clothes. Go somewhere to have fun. And, most importantly, take care of YOUR spiritual state. Attend a fellowship group.'

That brief conversation put me in a state of shock. Gradually, I began to understand that I no longer existed and lived the life of another person. I needed to find myself again. Of course, I didn't manage to do it right away, but I began to think about it.

Lorena, I'm telling you exactly the same thing. You need to see changes and you have to change. 'You have to start with yourself,'" Rita said.

It seemed that Lorena didn't expect such a turn of events.

"Why should I change? After all, he has the problems. It is he who is addicted, gets violent and can't find common ground with the children! It is he who is mocking me and swearing! After all he is taking drugs! And you say, 'Lorena, you need to change.' To change what? I earn money for the whole family, cook, clean, keep house and bring up the children!"

"That's it, it's time to change," Rita replied imperturbably, as if being unconscious of Lorena's tone and indignation.

"What? Do nothing? I'll starve to death together with the children. He won't do anything if I don't solve the problems," Lorena said with a raised voice.

"Do you think this is right?" Rita asked.

"No, I believe that he is a millstone around my neck. And moreover, he walks all over me. Do you even know how hard it is for me and what he does?" Lorena blurted out loud.

"That's exactly what I'm telling you. You know, Eleanor Roosevelt said, 'No one can make you feel inferior without your consent.' We aren't usually worried about what is happening to us, but about our voluntary consent for this to happen. Lorena, I definitely understand that this fact is very difficult to accept, especially if for a long time you have been attributing your misfortunes in the family to the behavior of your husband. But until a person can honestly and frankly say to themselves, 'I am what I am today because of the choices I made yesterday,' they can't say, 'I'm heading the other way.'"

And Lorena started crying and asked through her tears, "Is it my fault? Are you saying that I allowed him to treat me like this?"

"No, Lorena, I'm not saying that it's your fault. I just mean that if someone is a millstone around your neck, then this is your problem. Your neck is yours and the load of a millstone is also yours," explained Rita.

"A victim mentality is a way to avoid taking any responsibility for yourself or your life. You were betrayed, deceived and abused. Thus, you've become like a passive participant in your life.

Nothing depends on you, and therefore, you can't change anything. Such mentality is a dead end.

You feel sorry for yourself for having such a life. You feel sorry for your youth, which, as it seems to you, was stolen, as if everybody chose and made decisions instead of you.

You want someone to feel sorry for you, and when you tell someone about your life, you need people to sigh, groan and gasp, 'Poor thing, how hard it is for you! What a tyrant your husband is!' and the like. You are fuelled by the sympathy of other people. But if only someone says, 'Cheer up, don't worry! The best is yet to come,' and tells you how to get out of the problem, this person becomes your enemy, because they don't give what you want — sympathy.

You're trying to prove that you need sympathy, thinking, 'You don't understand me. I am doing much worse than it seems! Everything is hopeless.'

Look, Lorena! You just don't want to do and change anything. At the very least, you are ready to send your husband somewhere to be treated. It would be even better, if someone took care of him. You want everybody to stay out of the way and leave you alone. It's just comfortable for you to play the victim. You just enjoy feeling sorry for yourself. And if someone feels sorry for you too, that's just wonderful!"

"But how can one enjoy self-pity?" Lorena asked.

"It's quite simple. You feel sorry for yourself, people feel sorry for you, and you think, 'I'm really good, because I'm still alive somehow.' It raises your self-esteem and you consider yourself to be a hero. Self-pity is a sneaky 'friend'. It will pull you down deeper and deeper, until you are completely swallowed, incapable of thinking clearly and taking control over your life," declared Rita.

"I've been told such tough things for the first time. Before, people advised me to get divorced. They said I was an idiot to endure all of this. There is something in what you're saying. Are you typically so tough?" asked Lorena.

"No, I'm not! I'm tough only with people who ask such questions and are able, in my opinion, to handle such an answer. Moreover, I'm saying this without any conviction, because in the past I behaved exactly like that and went through the same thing. Can we continue?" Rita softened up and smiled.

"Oh, sure," agreed Lorena.

"Let's imagine that a mosquito had just landed on your hand, shoved its nose into your skin and had begun to drink your blood. You were watching how your blood was making it fat and you said, 'This mosquito has a problem. It behaves disorderly. It has no right to drink my blood! Why does it do this to me? Make it well! Take it to a rehabilitation center! Fix its brains and teach it that it's wrong to drink my blood.' It would be really weird and ridiculous to behave like that. Moreover, if that mosquito was taken to a rehab center, there would be a hundred more mosquitoes come in its place."

"My husband is a mosquito! That's why I want to swat him," Lorena laughed.

"No, your husband is not a mosquito," Rita smiled back, "I just can't find another example. A mosquito is a problem that attacks you, like depression, oppression, disappointment, or codependency on your husband's addiction. These 'mosquitoes' drink your blood, so first you need to sort your head out."

"And that's a thought! I'm no longer going to watch them sitting and drinking my blood. I'm going to kill them and drive them away," Lorena decided.

"Well done, but you will get tired of waving your hands in the air," Rita said.

"What should I do?" Lorena was diligent in her quest to find an answer.

"For example, if you use mosquito repellent, they won't even land on you, and there will be no need to deal with every one of them."

"Yes! Why didn't I figure that out?" Lorena said in quite a different mood, smiling. "This is really a very simple answer."

"That's just the point- that it's very simple. The Bible says that we are hidden with Christ in God. With Him we have protection from everything. Do you understand?"

"It turns out that if I'm with Him, mosquitoes won't get to me? "I'll see them, but they won't bite me, right?" asked Lorena.

"Yes, that's right," answered Rita confidently.

"You know, I'm starting to get it. I've realized that if I suffer, I have a problem. I didn't think about it before. It seemed to me that my husband was my problem, and when he would finally change, the problem would disappear. But now I see that even if he changes and frees my neck from the load, there will be someone else who becomes another millstone for me, if I don't change. It's like I'm trying to put a millstone on my neck and after that feel sorry for myself for having it there," Lorena concluded aloud and immediately continued, "It turns out that I either feel sorry for myself, thinking, 'Why is this happening to me?', or asking someone to do something with him. Okay, I'm going to change, but tell me how to do this? And what is my responsibility and what is he responsible for? What should I do? To stop cooking, cleaning up and working? Or to shout at him even louder than before as a response to his offenses? To kick him out of the apartment? Tell me what to do."

"And what did you do before?" Rita asked.

"I swore, cried, screamed, broke dishes, begged and pleaded. I was affectionate, kind and understanding. I helped and gave examples to him. Then I browbeat him, packed my things to leave, said that I would divorce, and cried again.... I've already tried everything. I've changed tactics and behavior, consulted with psychologists and friends, involved his parents and our children. I've done everything. What else is there?"

"Lorena, everything you are talking about are methods and actions. This is the outer shell and only a kind of game. I'm telling you to not just change your behavior, tactics and methods, but your heart, thoughts and inner determination. You want to receive a 'golden recipe'. You hope that someone tells you what to do and say and everything will change. Or that someone gives you a magic pill for him and he will be cured. But it's not like that. The Lord changes a person from within. The external things change as a result of internal changes. Do you understand me?"

"Yes, I understand, or think that I understand."

"You need to follow Christ. When you are in Christ, He is your shield. You need to understand what He has for you and how to live with that. You have to begin to study the Word of God. You can't change yourself, but God can, if you let Him, and He will do it with pleasure."

"Okay, I agree." Lorena stated.

As soon as they finished talking, the other girls began to come.

Vera brought a new girl to the group meeting.

"Everyone, this is Aliona, my classmate. We met by accident, and I invited her to us."

"Great, Aliona, we are glad to meet you!"

The girls also introduced themselves and, of course, tried to find out the reason why Aliona had come.

"To be honest, I don't know why I decided to come here. Vera invited me. I don't think that I have any problem. I've never been faced with drugs. But alcohol...," she was silent for a few seconds, "alcohol is normal for every family. As the saying goes, everybody drinks on special occasions and holidays. It's okay!"

"Are you married?" One of the girls asked, having interrupted Aliona.

"Yes, I am. My husband of course drinks a little, but I don't think he is an alcoholic. He doesn't lie around anywhere, but goes to work and earns money. Of course, it depends. He doesn't know when to stop and can get drunk on holidays. But how do we understand where the limit is? Is it normal or not? Everybody drinks. And he drinks too, because he gets tired at work. It seems to me that I blame him. I worry when he drinks. But he says that he has the right to relax."

"If you have any doubts whether or not it is normal, then this is an excuse to sort it out! Right, Rita?" Vera asked.

"Aliona, it's good that you came. If you have questions, then you need to find answers. After all, if nothing bothered you, you wouldn't wonder where the limit between occasional drinking and alcoholism was," said Rita.

"To be fair, I would like him to drink less, or, like all normal people, to not drink himself to death on holidays. But I can't understand what is right. What is normal for the family and how should I behave?" Aliona asked sincerely.

"Well, Aliona, you are in the right place. Vera has already told you that we study the Bible. The Word of God is like a mirror. When you listen to the Word and take heed to it, you see your life and your soul in the Word just like you can see your face in a mirror. When you look in a mirror, you see what to fix or how to brush your hair. It is hard to live without a mirror."

"That's right! When I look in a mirror and see that something is wrong with my hair, I know how to fix it. Is it true for the Bible?"

"Yes, it is! When you listen to sermons and read the Bible, your mind and thinking change. You start looking at things differently and begin to understand what and how to change."

"Once I tried reading the Bible, because I was curious, but there were only stories, so I didn't find anything that I could apply in my life," Aliona said.

"Therefore, you need to attend the fellowship group where we will study the Word, meditate on it and learn how to practically apply it in our lives," Rita replied.

"Rita, can you give us an example, please? So we can understand what it means to apply the Word in the life?"

"Sure! Since we've started talking about the Word, let's keep going.

God created everything through His Word. He said, 'Let there be light, and there was light.' Every time He created something, He spoke the Word, which became flesh.

He created the whole world by speaking WORDS!

This means that words have the power of creation.

Let's read from the Bible how God created the world.

> Then God said, "Let there be light"; and there was light. Then God said, "Let there be a firmament in the midst of the waters, and let it divide the waters from the waters." Then God said, "Let the waters under the heavens be gathered together into one place, and let the dry land appear"; and it was so.   ✒ Genesis 1:3, 6, 9

God created man in His image and according to His likeness. Man is the only creature on the earth that can speak. Just like God, you are able to create something with your words.

You can create your life with WORDS!

Let's remember the last week, for example. What kind of things did you created in your life over the last week?

If last week you called your husband a drug addict, an alcoholic, a bastard etc., was there anything good, in your opinion, that you created in your life and in the life of your husband?

By speaking such words, you curse your husband and affirm what is not true and what God didn't say for his life. You need to agree with God's words and affirm them.

God's Words carry life and power. These are not just words, because they are filled with God's Spirit. They carry the real power of God."

"Girls, I had a case a while back. I was very offended by a woman, and when we quarreled, I said to her within myself, 'I wish you were dead!' In a few days she died. I was tormented with remorse. Did she die because of me?"

"Vera, there is power in our words, but I can't answer your question. Maybe that woman was sick. We don't know everything about her life. But you need to ask God to forgive you for saying those words, and He will do this. And you have to forgive yourself too.

The Bible describes a case where an anointed prophet of God pronounced a curse and it came to pass. The closer a person gets to God, the stronger their words are. Therefore, we need to learn how to restrain mouth:

> Then he went up from there to Bethel; and as
> he was going up the road, some youths came
> from the city and mocked him, and said to him,
> "Go up, you baldhead! Go up, you baldhead!"
> So he turned around and looked at them,
> and pronounced a curse on them in the name
> of the Lord. And two female bears came out of
> the woods and mauled forty-two of the youths.
>
> ⤷ 2 Kings 2:23–24

The prophet cursed the youths, because they mocked and offended him. It's not written that God gave him such a task. It's not written that it was God's will. But the words of the prophet were powerful. Words have the power to bring life or death.

It is important to work on your character, in order to not say anything wrong within yourselves, because words really work. Especially since we are God's children. If the prophet had dealt with his resentment and hadn't said anything, the youths would've remained alive."

"Now I understand why God doesn't allow people to quickly take leadership positions, because before this, they must become mature in thought and words, so as to not cause harm, but to bring glory to God," said Lorena.

"Lorena, you're right. You don't assign leading positions to emotionally immature people in your company, right?"

"I don't. I've already had such an experience, and it didn't do any good. In that case, people made decisions based on their ambitions or resentment, instead of benefiting the group."

"Getting back to the subject, let me tell one more story. A short time ago I visited people whose son died from a drug overdose. But at that time their second son was still alive," Rita explained. "During our conversation with the father, he said many times that the second son would also die, and thus cursed his child. He did it because of anger and an inability to cope with the situation. We asked him not to speak like this and he apologized, but after a while he cursed his son again and again. It wasn't because he didn't love his second child. In fact, he didn't want his second son to die. Such words that curse allow the devil to work in the life of a person, because with curses, a person opens the door for unclean spirits.

After a short time, the second child also died, and also from a drug overdose.

I don't blame the father at all and I'm not saying that his son died because of him. The sons died from an overdose, but the father's words brought a curse into the lives of his children. The father didn't help them to get free from the addiction, but on the contrary, having the authority of a father, his spoken words caused harm to them.

Often you may hear parents telling their children, 'You're a loser! You're clumsy! You can't do anything!' Such words get into a person's soul very deeply, and subsequently it is very difficult for the person to live with. In adulthood, when this person starts a business or does something, they constantly hear the voice of their parents, saying, 'You are a loser!' and they believe it, because it was said by the father or the mother.

A child can't tell the difference between lies and the truth. They always believe their parents.

Also, wives curse their husbands, saying, 'Bloody fool, addict or alcoholic... Someday you'll drink yourself to death! You can't do anything. Your friends are losers!' I don't even want to list everything that the wives say.

With these words they try to change their husbands. But such words don't change for good and don't bring blessings, because they don't permit a person to rise above the situation. On the contrary, such words are like knives, deeply stabbing into the heart. They kill emotionally and spiritually, and subsequently we can see their results in the physical world.

Remember how Jesus cursed the fig tree and it withered? He showed us how powerful words are.

You can command illness or addiction to go away or wither up and die. But you never need to curse people.

God didn't give us the weapon of words to curse people, but with them we can bless and build our own lives and the lives of people.

Death and life are in the power of the tongue, so the Bible teaches us. It turns out that our words have enough power, and only we can decide what to say and what not to.

When scandals broke out in my family, I often locked myself in the bathroom and asked God to keep my tongue and help me to say nothing in anger.

The devil only expects us to start speaking evil words."

"I noticed," Alla said, "that during a scandal I say such things that make me scared. In fact, I don't want to do this and I don't think they're true, but this filth just flies out of my mouth. And then it just hurts."

"Rita, how can I be quiet if he calls me names?" Lorena continued the discussion. "He speaks to me such terrible words that I feel ashamed to repeat to you now. It turns out that he curses me, and because of him I have troubles."

"Look, the Bible also says that a curse without a cause shall not alight. You need to understand that you accepted Jesus, and that's why you aren't affected by any curse or magic. When you are in Jesus and take the right position before Him, you are fully protected," Rita replied.

"When my husband told me all sorts of nasty things, I used to be afraid. But having repented, I stopped being afraid, and every time I broke the power of those words in the Name of Jesus.

By saying bad words you allow unclean spirits to control the life of your husband.

God's words are so strong that when He commands something to appear, it appears, and when He commands something to wither, it withers. If you agree with God's Words and declare them over your life, your life will begin to change according to His Words."

"Well then, what can I speak?" Lorena asked.

"Let's read the first Psalm:

> Blessed is the man Who walks not in the counsel of the ungodly, nor stands in the path of sinners, nor sits in the seat of the scornful; but his delight is in the law of the Lord, and in His law he meditates day and night. He shall be like a tree planted by the rivers of water that brings forth its fruit in its season, whose leaf also shall not wither; and whatever he does shall prosper.
>
> ∽ Psalm 1:1–3

You can declare these words over the life of your husband. Look, it says here that blessed is the man, and it means that this person is incredibly and constantly happy.

Lorena, you can say these words about your husband. That your husband is blessed, that he doesn't follow the advice of the ungodly and doesn't spend time with them. That he doesn't sit in the seat of the scornful. It means he doesn't go to drug dens or similar places. Declare that in His law your husband meditates day and night. It means he thinks about God's will for his life and consults God about everything. Say that you husband is like a tree which is not wild, but planted by God with love. That this tree is planted by the rivers of water and doesn't wither, because it feeds on the fresh water of God. That this tree brings forth its fruit in its season. It means your husband serves God and brings forth fruit. He will be able to do everything. He will work and earn money. That the leaf of this tree shall not wither. It means that your husband will be full of strength. That whatever he does, he shall prosper and succeed.

When you read these words of God, take heed to their meaning and declare them over your husband. This is God's Word, which has real power. Let your mouth speak God's words. Just as God created this world and everything in it by the Word, His words will create a new life for you and your husband. God stands by His Word and brings it into action. Do you understand?"

"Rita, I do. I need to take heed to the Word, understand and declare it over my life and the life of my husband, and so it will be."

"Yes, Lorena, so it will be. When you read the Bible, God will reveal to you other details of His Word. You will understand and speak it out in prayer."

CHAPTER 3

Don't Control Him!
It Doesn't Work!

Lorena was obviously out of sorts. She flew into the room like lightning, and even forgot to say hello.

Rita and Vera were having tea together.

"Hello, Lorena! Has someone parked their car the wrong way again?" Vera asked jokingly.

"Oh, men really don't know how to park a car, do they, Lorena? Have you taught them how to do it?" The girls smiled. But, for sure, Lorena was in a bad mood.

"Why are you kidding me? I fail to see what's so funny. I'm not in the mood, okay?"

"Okay! Would you like some tea?" they asked her.

"No, thanks."

"Well, tell us, what's going on? You flew into the room and didn't even say hello," Rita asked.

"And what's going on is that I'm already sick and tired of all this! I just was at the pawnshop and sold the gold ring my mother gave me. I'm so tired of keeping control of everything. I'm tired of constantly selling something to the pawnshop. I'm tired of bailing him out of jail. I can't take any more of this. I have to find him a job and pay for his problems, but he doesn't even say thanks. He doesn't want to hear from me! If he can't think for himself, he could at least do what he is told. He got involved with his old friend and is hanging out with him now. I've been trying to get ahold of him for three hours, but his phone is out of range. I need him to go to my mother and pick up something. I think it's all over with him. If it goes on this way, I will file for divorce and he will never see his child. The child doesn't need such a father."

"Lorena, why do you do this? Why are you selling the pawned items? Let him solve his own problems," Vera said.

"He will never solve them! Should I wait until he comes to his senses? But if I do so, I will lose the furniture, TV set and everything else."

Vera's phone rang.

"Girls, I'm going to meet Aliona near the subway station," Vera said.

"Ok, Vera! While we're waiting for you, we're going to talk," Rita said. "Dear Lorena, if you solve a person's problems, you constantly shield them from the consequences of their own actions. That's why your husband can't realize how serious they are. Just think! Why does he have to change something, if you do everything for him? You don't give your husband the opportunity to decide what to do with his life," Rita continued.

"Excellent! And what about my life? I can't wait! Time is going by and I'm not getting any younger," Lorena retorted.

"You have to take good care of yourself and your life."

"I don't get it. Don't I take care of myself? I'll be fine, as soon as he quits drugs."

"You're not living your life, but your husband's life. You constantly control his whole life and every step he takes."

"Yes, I do, because he's worse than a baby."

"But, if you control his life, you won't give God the opportunity to work with him and to set him free."

"But what am I doing wrong? I only want the best for him. I've dedicated my life to him."

"Look what's happening. You are trying to abolish the law of sowing and reaping in his life. And this is wrong. The Bible says: 'For whatever a man sows, that he will also reap.' You aren't letting him realize what his actions lead to. Let's imagine, for a second, that your husband was a farmer...."

"It looks like the truth, but his only occupation related to the farming business was growing hemp and mushrooms at home. I had to shut down his small business," Lorena retorted.

"You see, you don't give him a chance to develop! Just kidding," Rita said, and continued her imaginary story, "So, your husband was a farmer. Some time ago he had sold all the seeds of wheat that he had. There had been nothing left for planting and, of course, he hadn't planted anything. Harvest time came, and he had a wonderful harvest because while he was spending the money he'd gotten from selling the seeds on drinking, you had bought new seeds and worked on the field day and night. And this went on for years. It was obvious that he didn't have to even think about the harvest for the next year, and he didn't have to do anything about it. He didn't even stop to think that he couldn't spend the money received from selling the seeds on drinking. That's exactly what is happening. You don't take drugs, but you are exhausted, because you constantly redeem the pawned things, while he takes drugs and doesn't care about how to pick them up from the pawnshop. You took the responsibility which is not yours, and that's why it's so hard for you. Take on your part of the responsibility and let your husband take his. Also, give your husband to the Lord because only God can deal with him."

"I don't quite understand. Does this mean that I don't have to solve all these problems?"

"That's right! You don't. Maybe, he needs to realize that if he sells his cell phone in the pawnshop and doesn't redeem it, he wouldn't have a cell phone. Or, if he didn't go to work because of a spree, he would be fired. But you cover up for him to the boss, saying that he got sick. It turns out that you are lying to people. And he is not fired, although he skips work. You don't need to say anything to his boss. Let him solve his own problems at work. It's very simple: if he skips work again, he will be fired."

"You make it sound so easy. Well, how do you think everything will change? If I am quiet, our apartment will be empty, he won't have a job and probably won't even change clothes or take a shower."

"The question isn't how to change everything, or how to change your husband, but how you can change to please the Lord. God Himself will deal with your husband, when you do your part. Your job is to pray for him and do what the Word of God says. And God will show you how to solve all the problems."

"Oh, Rita, I don't understand."

"Look, you've already done everything that you could, and it doesn't work at all. Now try another way. You know, many addicted people don't want to go to a rehab center or undergo treatment, because they are 'fine'. They still have a job and there is the impression that everything's alright, artificially created by their mothers and wives. But when a person is out of a job and runs out of money, they realize that they have to change something and agree to be sent to a rehab center."

"What a wonderful idea! I'm going to call his boss tonight and ask to fire him. Once I helped Hena, so I think he won't refuse doing me a favor. He will probably even be glad to get rid of Kostia."

"No, you don't have to do this. You are trying to deal with this on your own again. You just want to take control over him and force him to do what is convenient for you."

"I don't understand you! One second you are saying that I don't have to help him and the next that I have to!"

"Don't try to keep everything under your control. You aren't helping your husband this way.

God created man and gave him a free will, so He respects his will. When we keep everything under our control, we don't let God into our lives. Until we give up control, God won't solve our problems.

It looks like you are telling God, 'Everything is under my control, and I'm going to solve this problem on my own.' If you were told the same thing, you would also just stand by. God says, 'Dear Lorena, I respect your decision, and if you need My help, I'm here, just call Me.'

God doesn't have ready-made formulas to deal with different situations, nor does He use all of the same ways to solve different problems. He heals different people in different ways. He is a living God. Jesus healed two blind men in completely different ways: one of them was healed through a simple touch and the other one in a quite strange way.

Jesus spat on the ground and made clay with the saliva; and He anointed the eyes of the blind man with the clay. God isn't predictable. You need to trust Him and try to change yourself, but not someone else. You can't make God act as you want.

Let's turn to the Word of God, because without it we won't be able to do anything. Let's try to figure out what we should do.

> Then they sailed to the country of the Gadarenes, which is opposite Galilee. And when He stepped out on the land, there met Him a certain man from the city who had demons for a long time. And he wore no clothes, nor did he live in a house but in the tombs. When he saw Jesus, he cried out, fell down before Him, and with a loud voice said, "What have I to do with You, Jesus, Son of the Most High God? I beg You, do not torment me!" For He had commanded the unclean spirit to come out of the man. For it had often seized him, and he was kept under guard, bound with chains and shackles; and he broke the bonds and was driven by the demon into the wilderness. Jesus asked him, saying, "What is your name?" And he said, "Legion," because many demons had entered him. And they begged Him that He would not command them to go out into the abyss. Now a herd of many swine was feeding there on the mountain. So they begged Him that He would permit them to

enter them. And He permitted them. Then the demons went out of the man and entered the swine, and the herd ran violently down the steep place into the lake and drowned. When those who fed them saw what had happened, they fled and told it in the city and in the country. Then they went out to see what had happened, and came to Jesus, and found the man from whom the demons had departed, sitting at the feet of Jesus, clothed and in his right mind. And they were afraid. They also who had seen it told them by what means he who had been demon-possessed was healed. Then the whole multitude of the surrounding region of the Gadarenes asked Him to depart from them, for they were seized with great fear. And He got into the boat and returned. Now the man from whom the demons had departed begged Him that he might be with Him. But Jesus sent him away, saying: "Return to your own house, and tell what great things God has done for you." And he went his way and proclaimed throughout the whole city what great things Jesus had done for him.   ⌁ Luke 8:26–39

That demon-possessed man suffered from his primary problem, but there was also an additional problem — people who wanted to help him.

Relatives who were near to him tried to help him the way they thought was suitable and right.

...For it had often seized him, and he was kept under guard, bound with chains and shackles;

and he broke the bonds and was driven by the demon into the wilderness.   ∽ Luke 8:29

Those people were his family, but they bound their loved one with chains and shackles so he wouldn't run to the tombs.

However, since the demon tortured him and drove him into the wilderness, the demon-possessed man couldn't sit down, still being bound. What happened? He broke the bonds and ran away. Undoubtedly, when he broke those bonds, his arms and legs were wounded and bled. He couldn't sit still. And the tighter he was bound, the deeper and more painful wounds he had. That lasted for not just a few days, but for a long time.

Such 'care' didn't help him to recover, but only aggravated the problem and caused additional pain. Today the same things happen. The husbands are locked in the apartments, but they run out through the windows, risking their lives, or break down the doors, causing damage to themselves and their relatives."

"Rita, while you were speaking, I remembered something," Vera interrupted her. "Can I tell you?"

"Yes, please tell us, but only if it goes along with the point."

"I had a neighbor. Once his wife locked him in the apartment, so that he couldn't go to his friends and drink together with them. So he decided to get out of that prison through the balcony of his neighbor. They lived on the eleventh floor. When he was climbing over the wall between their balconies, he couldn't find a place to put his foot, looked down and fell to his death. His wife couldn't save her husband. She suffered so much that he died because of her."

"She did her best to save him. She wasn't to blame for her husband's death. His alcoholism killed him. This craving, this addiction, this demon simply drives a person into the wilderness, so that they struggle in every possible way and flee. She wanted to help her husband, but it's impossible to release a person by controlling them."

"Rita, does this mean that I don't have to lock my husband in the apartment? He is unruly. What if he leaves the apartment and doesn't return. But on the other hand, if I lock him in, he may try to escape and hurt himself. It turns out that I don't have to help him, or what?"

"Control is **imposing** your help on a person, who **didn't ask** for it. Control is having an obsessive desire to rule your husband. You see, you behave as if you are God and you know better what to do or say, and how to live or act. As a result, a person doesn't live their own life, but you, as a savior, lead them through life and control their actions. This is wrong. God gave a free will to everyone.

A person may be bound not only with chains and shackles, but also with words and deeds. For example, by reminding a person that they're going to die, if they don't quit the addiction, we not only fail to stop them, but also do additional harm. Such words and arguments don't stop a person, but offer the demons an opportunity to torment them even more.

You do 'good deeds' for your husband, save him from all his troubles and problems, and then wonder why he doesn't say thank you. You think he is just so ungrateful!

But in fact, he is not ungrateful. It is you who are sticking your nose where it doesn't belong. Therefore, instead of being grateful, your husband is rude to you.

But at the same time, it is okay to help if you are asked to do that.

For example, the husband of one of our friends asked her to lock him in the apartment for the purpose of helping him. That is no longer control. He knew that he wouldn't be able to resist the temptation to buy drugs, so he asked his wife to help. He told her not to let him go, even if he pleaded. This is real help. But if a person isn't even going to stop drinking and someone locks them in the apartment by force, this is control.

Of course, when a person is delusional (for example, is in intensive care, when they need to be saved), they are not consulted, because in such a state they are unable to make decisions, in contrast to the case where they undergo planned treatment. If a person has been drinking hard for a long time, it may happen that they won't be able to stop drinking without help. But it's dangerous to make them stop drinking right away and simply lock them in the apartment. It is necessary to consult a doctor and call an ambulance. I don't mean that you have to renounce and ignore the addict. But you can't control their will and life. If you control someone, it means that you don't have your own life or your life is completely consumed by their addiction. You need to become free from control. In such a way, you will help yourself and you will have your own life.

One day when I was praying, I imagined my husband bound with chains and shackles and trying to get free from them. I saw that he was exhausted by drugs, debts and a negative attitude towards himself. He was so sick and tired of such a life that he already hated himself. No one was able to tame him and help. No one was able to put up with him and his trouble.

I saw myself in that story. I was the one who bound him with chains and shackles, and caused him unbearable pain. He had already been wounded, but those chains and shackles gave him more pain. He tore off those chains, and as a result his arms and legs were wounded and bled. Before, I didn't understand that when I tried to control a person, even for good reasons (to save, to rescue and to help), I caused them additional pain and made them suffer. I cried, because I was so sorry for controlling him and for making things worse.

But I was inspired by the fact that there was Jesus who could help. My husband needed Jesus, because He was certainly able to help him. Just as I needed Jesus to come to my family and liberate us from that misfortune, so you need Him now, Lorena."

"I'm beginning to understand," Lorena said. "I need to pray for my husband to meet Jesus. Jesus knows how to release him. I feel guilty because I always controlled my husband, checked his notes, removed SMS messages, and always told him what to do."

"Just ask God to forgive you and help to change your behavior. Every time you feel the desire to control him, just try to change it. Focus on your own life, your relationship with God and your heart before Him. Study the Scriptures, pray and grow in God and do something for Him. But as for your husband, just put him in God's hands."

"Oh, Rita, I think it's too early for him to be put in God's hands. He has really worked my nerves, but I'll let him live," Lorena joked.

"Oh, Lorena, you just want to turn everything into a joke. Okay, let's study the Word."

"Okay! I really want to change. I think I can do this."

"Sure, you can, if you have such an attitude. If I could do this and the girls could do this, you will also be able to do this. For the Almighty God is with you.

> So Abraham rose early in the morning, and took bread and a skin of water; and putting it on her shoulder, he gave it and the boy to Hagar, and sent her away. Then she departed and wandered in the Wilderness of Beersheba. And the water in the skin was used up, and she placed the boy under one of the shrubs. Then she went and sat down across from him at a distance of about a bowshot; for she said to herself, "Let me not see the death of the boy." So she sat opposite him, and lifted her voice and wept. And God heard the voice of the lad. Then the angel of God called to Hagar out of heaven, and said to her, "What ails you, Hagar? Fear not, for God has heard the voice of the lad where he is. Arise, lift up the lad and hold him with your hand, for I will make him a great nation." Then God opened her eyes, and she saw a well of water. And she went and filled the skin with water, and gave the lad a drink. So God was with the lad; and he grew and dwelt in the wilderness, and became an archer. ࣷ Genesis 21:14–20

While Hagar was near her son, the son counted on her help. His mother took care of him and solved all his problems. His mother was looking for water. The mother was like a god to him. Sometimes we do the same thing to our relatives. But when his mother stepped aside, he had no choice but to ask help from the Almighty God. When the son asked for help from God, God answered him. Then the Lord told Hagar that He heard the voice of the lad. All that time God waited for there to be no one standing between Him and the lad. God doesn't need mediators in communication, because God deals with every one of us personally. We can ask God on behalf of a person, as well as pray for this person and help them, but we don't have to stand between this person and God. Before that, Ishmael didn't need to ask anything from God, because his mother did everything for him. But a person can't do what only God can do. Our care and help don't have to be the barrier between God and a person. Sometimes we try to be a savior, without even thinking that we can't do this, and that a person themself has to call the Lord into their own life.

Hagar felt so much pain at the sight of her son that she could no longer watch him die. You experience the same pain when you see your husband dying from drugs and can't do anything. You've already tried everything. You've seen all the doctors together with him. He's been treated by medicines. You've asked and persuaded him. You've manipulated and frightened him. You've threatened to divorce him. You've driven away his friends. You've been to every monastery. But nothing has helped. He is getting worse and worse. More and more he needs living water, but you don't know where to find it and what to do. Therefore, Hagar departed from her son, because she had already done everything she could, and appealed to God. In order for the Lord to be able to help our family members, we can't control their lives, but allow God to show them His way out.

There was a case that the wife of an addict attended our group and had been praying for him. That woman controlled him terribly. Once her husband communicated with one minister and agreed to meet him and talk. It was a big breakthrough because before, he didn't believe that they could help him and didn't want any help at all. The guy asked that his relatives didn't know about that meeting.

When the wife found out that the minister communicated with her husband, she created a scandal and decided to not come to the group anymore. Things got out of her control. She wanted to control her husband's treatment. She believed that only she had the right to decide whether or not her husband could meet with someone, and she thought that she knew the best words for him and the best way for him to be set free.

Control is the devil's method of preventing a person from becoming free.

Let's look at one more story from the Bible.

> While He spoke these things to them, behold, a ruler came and worshiped Him, saying, "My daughter has just died, but come and lay Your hand on her and she will live." So Jesus arose and followed him, and so did His disciples. And suddenly, a woman who had a flow of blood for

twelve years came from behind and touched the hem of His garment. For she said to herself, "If only I may touch His garment, I shall be made well." But Jesus turned around, and when He saw her He said, "Be of good cheer, daughter; your faith has made you well." And the woman was made well from that hour. When Jesus came into the ruler's house, and saw the flute players and the noisy crowd wailing, He said to them, "Make room, for the girl is not dead, but sleeping." And they ridiculed Him. But when the crowd was put outside, He went in and took her by the hand, and the girl arose. And the report of this went out into all that land. When Jesus departed from there, two blind men followed Him, crying out and saying, "Son of David, have mercy on us!"

৩ Matthew 9:18–27

The daughter of that father was dying at home. She was very ill. Her parents most likely tried to help her in all possible ways. But in order to really help her, her father had to leave her and go looking for Jesus.

Sometimes, instead of staying with your husband and guarding him, you will have to leave everything and go seeking God. To seek Him in the Word, in prayer and in sermons. Because Jesus is the only solution. The girl's father found Jesus and brought Him to his home. While the father was looking for God, his daughter died, and he could say, 'Well, when I left, she died, and I wasn't around.' But He believed God. Jesus came to his house and brought life to his daughter.

When the problem is more than you can handle, or your family member is on the verge of life and death, you have to leave everything and go looking for Jesus. And to do this, you have to get out of the atmosphere of despair, because you don't need to become infected with despair and reconcile yourself to the circumstances. You have to go and find Jesus, because only He is able to solve your problem. The father didn't take the wife, other relatives and even the daughter with him. It may happen that you can't bring your husband or your relatives to the church, to the group, to the doctor, or to someone who can help. In such a case you need to get out of that atmosphere of mess, despair, suffering and pain, find Jesus and bring Him to your home. What does this mean? It means that being at home in the atmosphere of despair, you can't change anything. It means that the blind can't lead the blind. It means that when your faith is at zero level and you are in despair, you can't help your husband. You need to leave everything and come to the group and to the church service. You need to read the Word of God. It is necessary to seek Jesus in prayer at home. Perhaps, in order to pray, you will need to go to the bathroom and lock the door. You need to do everything possible to just find Jesus, worship Him and ask Him to come and heal your husband.

You can't find the way to solve the problem in your family, unless you step outside this problem."

CHAPTER 4

Learn to Say No

During the group meeting Lorena's phone rang. She turned off the sound, but the phone didn't stop ringing. Lorena left the room to talk. It was her husband, who once again had had an accident. In a short period of time, it was his seventh accident.

Lorena was afraid to take the car from him. It seemed that she had enough courage to do something, but she really couldn't deal with her husband. She didn't seem to understand how dangerous it was. He often fell asleep at the wheel or was distracted by an SMS message for a second. As he read the message for too long, car accidents happened. Lorena was in a daze. She understood how dangerous it was and didn't understand it at the same time. She had long been confused about what was right or wrong.

Her husband's driving in such a state could invoke danger and death for not only him, but also other people, pedestrians and other drivers. But Lorena preferred to hide behind her pain and to not look at the situation objectively.

"Dear Lorena, I've had an accident. The police are going to take my car, and the head of the Municipal Traffic Police has arrived. The girl who crashed into me is a daughter of some bigwig. I need two thousand dollars or my car will get towed. They've already taken my driver's license."

"Ok, let them take it! Later we'll deal with that."

"You don't understand! We will have to pay for each day the car spends at the tow. And they will try to make sure that we can't take it from there too quickly. Peter's car has already been there for six months. They don't allow us to just take it. And all the tires have already been stolen."

"I'm not giving you any money. Let them take it. I'm sick of this!" For the first time, Lorena had the inner strength to say "no" and to not rush to solve her husband's problems. God had made big changes inside of her during her time in church and at the fellowship group, and the support of her new friends and Rita gave her strength and confidence.

Lorena hung up and told Rita what had happened. But for just an instant Lorena thought, "Maybe I should really give him money, because later it's going to be more expensive." But Rita advised her to be strong and to finally stop paying for all of the troubles that her husband constantly got into.

"Lorena, it's time for him to see the consequences of his actions. You have to understand that it is very dangerous to drive in such a condition. He has to realize the gravity of the situation. Thank God that everyone is still alive."

The girls immediately began to pray for Lorena's husband and asked God to keep him safe and to help in solving this situation.

Then he called again.

"Lorena, don't you understand? They will forge the tests and say that I was drunk. We might lose the car."

"You know, the car is not the most important thing in life. I've already told you no. Let them execute the infringement notice and take the car and the license. You will come to your senses and will solve this problem later."

It was Lorena's big victory. She would no longer be an accomplice and a lifeguard. She would no longer redeem the pawned things. She would no longer buy new phones so that her husband could be in touch. She would no longer cover for him before his boss. She would no longer lie to his parents.

It was time to change.

The phone rang again. This time it was her husband's friend.

"Lorena, he's asking me to give him money."

"I'm not going to pay you back. Don't give him money, please."

But the friend couldn't refuse him. Being a real friend, he decided to help. But he didn't even realize that he had done him a disservice. He couldn't leave his friend in trouble. Even his wife hadn't come to the rescue, but he was a friend. 'A friend in need is a friend indeed'. It was important that everybody come together to solve the problem. If everyone does what only they think is right, the addict then continues to manipulate and play his game.

When Lorena arrived home, her husband was not there yet. He came later. He was extremely upset.

"Lorena, you left me. You betrayed me."

"No, I didn't betray you. And don't try to make me feel guilty. You had an accident being under the influence of drugs and demanded several thousand dollars out of the family budget to solve the problem caused by your taking drugs."

"I didn't take anything."

"Don't lie to me! That's enough."

Later Lorena learned the full truth. Her husband was driving in a state of drug intoxication and was going to buy another dose. On the curve he fell asleep, clipped a double white line, slammed into oncoming traffic and crashed into a car. That situation was a big stress to him and after that, he thought about many things. He became scared for himself. It wasn't the last day of drug use, but it was an important point in his soul searching.

CHAPTER 5

Get Rid of Shame

The fellowship group had already started, and everyone was present. Suddenly Vera began to cry.

"Girls, I can't stand it anymore. I live in constant shame and fear. At work I'm afraid that they will find out my husband's problem. What if he suddenly comes to work in such a condition? I'm embarrassed to go to my parents. They already miss me, call, invite and ask us to come. When they see him, they will immediately understand that he is a drug addict. In the mornings, when I go out to work, I try not to make eye contact with my neighbors. I pretend that I don't notice my husband's condition. What should I do? How do I live with this? I'm terribly ashamed of him, and even more of myself being with him. It's terrible."

"I understand you, Vera. Let's see what is written in the Word of God," Rita said.

"Ok," Vera said through the tears. Lorena sat next to Vera and embraced her, although such an expression of endearment was very unusual for Lorena. Vera was deeply touched by Lorena's embrace and the fact that somebody actually understood her, so the tears streamed down her face even more. For about five minutes, Vera couldn't calm down, but after having a good cry, she said,

"I'm so lucky to have you. It's great to know that I'm not alone, and that there is someone who understands me."

Rita broke the silence and announced what they were going to talk about.

"I want to tell you something. Once I read the story of the demon-possessed man from the country of the Gadarenes."

"We talked about him recently," Lorena remembered.

"It's good that you remember. Let's read this story again and look at it from another point of view.

> Then they sailed to the country of the Gadarenes, which is opposite Galilee. And when He stepped out on the land, there met Him a certain man from the city who had demons for a long time. And he wore no clothes, nor did he live in a house but in the tombs. When he saw Jesus, he cried out, fell down before Him, and with a loud voice said, "What have I to do with You, Jesus, Son of the Most High God? I beg You, don't torment me!" For He had commanded the unclean spirit to come out of the man. For it had often seized him, and he was kept under guard, bound with chains and shackles; and he broke the bonds and was driven by the demon into the wilderness.   ∾ Luke 8:26–29

Look, girls! That man was demon-possessed. Demons tormented him and forced him to do what he didn't want to do.

> *For what I am doing, I do not understand. For what I will to do, that I do not practice; but what I hate, that I do.*

> For the good that I will to do, I do not do; but the evil I will not to do, that I practice. Now if I

do what I will not to do, it is no longer I who do it, but sin that dwells in me.

        Romans 7:15, 19–20

I often hear from you and from other wives, 'He has to pull himself together and endure.' I'm sure that that demon-possessed man tried to pull himself together and endure many times, but it didn't work. A person can't be in their own hands. They are either in the hands of God, who strengthens, guides and helps them, or in the hands of the devil, who enslaves them.

Often, when we ask a person why they did something, they can't even answer. They say, 'I don't know how it happened. I didn't want to do it.' And they aren't lying.

Why did the demon-possessed man behave so badly? The demons made him to do it. The addict is enslaved by demons, and they manipulate him like a puppet in a puppet theater. No matter how hard he tries to do otherwise, he just can't. The demons attack his body, his mind and his life. That demon-possessed man didn't want to live in the tombs and run around without clothes, revealing his shame. It's the same thing that happens to the addict. If we think about it, we can understand that he doesn't want to be beaten by the demons, spend nights in the drug dens or on the streets, or bring himself to an early death and show his problem to everyone. Clothing is our veil, and it covers our nakedness. The fact that the demon-possessed man wore no clothes tells us that he couldn't hide his condition. A person in a state of drug or alcohol intoxication isn't able to cover up their sin. There comes a time when it becomes obvious for relatives, neighbors, friends and acquaintances. Just think, what did the relatives of that demon-possessed man feel? Shame. I think, even great shame. You can feel the same today.

If your husbands are in such a condition, you are ashamed that people see it. But don't despair. This problem can be solved, and Jesus is able to do it.

As soon as Jesus freed that man from demons, he came to his senses and became completely sane. At one time, the will of that man was broken, but Jesus set him free. And finally he was able to do what he wanted, and resist what he didn't want.

Why did the demons make him live in the tombs? Because this is the place where people are dead, spiritually dead, and where there is no life. What does it mean to live at home? Our home is our fortress, our protection. When we are at home, we feel safe and can relax. We are at home when we are with the Lord. We are at home when we are spiritually alive.

When a person sins, they pull away from God and hide from Him. If your husband, for example, used to go to church and talked to people there with pleasure, and now he doesn't want to communicate with believers and tries to avoid them, it's a sign that something is wrong. Even if you don't notice that something is wrong with him, begin to pray for him more intensely.

There is an interesting thing related to this story. People saw that their neighbor, brother, son, or friend was healed, but instead of being happy for him, they were frightened. After all, he became free and sane. He stopped beating his head against the wall, screaming and running naked. He was clothed and in his right mind, and also felt good. It was a real miracle. Before he was dying, was driven by the demons, spent nights in the tombs, beat his head against the rocks, screamed incomprehensibly and ran naked, but nobody was scared. But as soon as he became free, everyone became frightened because of Jesus's power which was stronger than a legion of demons.

When your husbands become drug or alcohol free, not everyone will clap their hands and run to church with you. It won't be like that. Some people may react negatively. They may be frightened by Jesus's power, which is stronger than drugs. They will ask you to not speak about the Lord. People are always afraid of what they don't know. Don't be upset and don't give up. Jesus told the man from the country of the Gadarenes to go and preach. Jesus never assigns the hopeless tasks. He will be with you, and many people will be healed and set free through you."

"Oh, I wish he would get free," Lorena said. "I already don't care what people think. If only my husband would be healed."

"But I do care! I don't want people to point at me and talk about my life behind my back."

"Oh, people will always talk. Do you really think that if your husband is free, they will stop talking? They will find another reason."

"Lorena, they can talk about my shoes or something else, but not about this. It's a painful subject."

"Oh, Rita, sorry! We are ignoring the point again."

"Well, let's look at another story from the Bible. I think that the woman we're going to talk about now also didn't like that people were talking about her. But after discussing her story, we are going to receive healing, just like by looking at your life, someone will come to Jesus.

> Now a certain woman had a flow of blood for twelve years, and had suffered many things from many physicians. She had spent all that she had and was no better, but rather grew worse. When she heard about Jesus, she came behind Him in the crowd and touched His garment. For she said, "If only I may touch His clothes, I shall be made well." Immediately the fountain of her blood was dried up, and she felt in her body that she was healed of the affliction. And Jesus, immediately knowing in Himself that power had gone out of Him, turned around in the crowd and said, "Who touched My clothes?"   ❦ Mark 5:25–30

She had a very shameful and intimate problem. She had a flow of blood that wouldn't stop. Because of that problem, she had no right to communicate with people, and I don't think that anyone even wanted to talk with her. And even if people wanted to communicate with her, they couldn't because of other people's opinions. Does this seem familiar to you? No one wants to communicate with people who have shameful problems, such as alcoholism or drug addiction. Most likely, people discuss them behind their backs or even point at them. But the woman didn't care about that. She didn't listen to those stupid things, because she was interested in Jesus. Why? Because He was the solution to her shameful problem.

You know, when she secretly touched Jesus's garment, it was just one touch, but it required great courage. After that, it took courage to admit that she had done it. The woman had to overcome her shame. Jesus asked who had touched Him, and the woman had to respond before everyone, 'It's me, the one who had a flow of blood, the one who had a shameful problem.' That was a problem that she couldn't talk about. This problem had made her unclean. But she was able to overcome her fear and was healed.

It doesn't matter what people think. It is important that Jesus is able to heal everyone.

You don't have to justify yourself to anyone. You don't have to explain anything to anyone. You don't need to hide your head. You are not guilty of anything and you have nothing to be ashamed of. Yes, you have a problem, but no one has the right to condemn you. Jesus doesn't condemn you.

You will not be ashamed because you trust in the Lord.

Many people hide their problems, because they are ashamed to talk about them. Because of this, their problems are not solved for years. But you can reveal your problem and solve it. Then there will be no 'flow of blood'.

You know, girls, I'm proud of you. No matter what, you come here and open up about your problems. That's admirable. That is a big step to success.

Dear Vera, you need to get rid of shame, and this doesn't mean that you need to share your problems to everyone and complain. Not at all. You just don't need to be ashamed, because the Lord will help you to deal with this. You won't be afraid to look your neighbors in the eyes anymore. You won't worry that at work people might find out about your problem.

You know, shame is such a thing that never goes anywhere on its own. When your husband becomes free, there will be another reason for shame. For example, you will be ashamed to tell people that you're a believer or to refuse to drink at work. Or you will be ashamed that at some event you are dressed differently than other people. Shame can change its form. Therefore, you have to get rid of shame, and to not wait until your husband becomes a super hero and everyone starts to envy you.

Even if suddenly your husband becomes a super hero, people will begin to wonder what a man like him sees in such a woman like you. As a result, you may be ashamed again that there's something wrong with you. The problem is not your husband, but the shame, which you don't need.

Do you know when the first time was that shame came into being? The moment when people first sinned. And in order to cover up their shame, they decided to sew leaves together and make themselves clothes. But such clothes couldn't cover them, so God gave them clothes of skin. An innocent animal had to suffer to cover up the shame of people.

Jesus died in the most shameful way — by crucifixion. He took such a punishment to take away our shame and the shame of our families. When Jesus was crucified, He was naked and ashamed. People laughed at Him and mocked Him, saying that He needed to come down from the cross and save Himself. But He tolerated all of the mocking and torments, because He knew that He would gain a great victory. At that time, He already knew that you wouldn't be able to get through this. He knew that you wouldn't be able to help yourself. You have to admit that it's silly to pay for goods in a store if your friend already paid for them, received a check and gave them to you for free. It is foolish to feel ashamed before people, if Jesus has already paid for your freedom. Just accept this gift and tell Him 'THANK YOU'. He did this because of His great love for you. He allowed His nakedness to be revealed. He overcame shame, when everyone looked at Him, humiliated Him and spat on Him. He seemed to be defenseless. He was disfigured. He tolerated all of that in order for you to be free from shame and disgrace.

Let's pray together. Who of you wants to be delivered from shame by Jesus? I'm going to lead you in prayer. So repeat after me and understand what you are praying for:

> Lord Jesus, You took my shame upon Yourself, so that I wouldn't be ashamed. You let them undress You when you were crucified. Everyone looked at Your nakedness and mocked You. You voluntarily let it happen so that I could be free from shame. I accept this exchange and thank You for this sacrifice! From this day on, the shame of my husband's behavior will no longer have power over me, and I will walk with my head held high. I have nothing more to be ashamed of. You are My Lord! Amen!"

As it turned out, everyone prayed. More or less that was true for every woman present at the group meeting. After all, every one of the women had to step back into the unpleasant situations because of their husband's behavior. And everyone was ashamed to have such a husband.

After the prayer, Rita continued,

"Don't be ashamed of the behavior of your loved ones and don't be ashamed of yourself. Don't hide, but trust the Lord.

After Jesus healed the demon-possessed man, he was already clothed, because there was no shame anymore. He was already in his right mind.

The woman became healthy and had no flow of blood anymore. God gave Adam and Eve the clothes of skin. And there was nothing anyone could say to them because old things had passed away and all things had become new. And the most important thing is that Jesus delivered them and us from shame."

CHAPTER 6

Get Rid of Fear

In the summer, the girls took a break from the meetings. Each one spent the summer differently. One of them traveled to their summer house, someone else to the sea, and another to the city. Rita had just returned from vacation. Everyone had gotten a bit of a rest and a tan.

Upon meeting, the girls embraced. They had missed each other during the break.

"Well, how did you spend the summer?" Rita asked.

The girls began to share impressions of their vacations. They asked Rita how she had spent her time.

"I decided to go diving. And, you know, I learnt something about my life.

When I was already underwater, I suddenly started to panic and became frightened. And I began to suffocate, not because there wasn't enough air, but because of fear.

I start making signals to the coach to take me out of the water. In fact, there was no real danger. All the equipment worked properly and there was enough air. However, I got a little water under the mask, but sometimes that happens, and we were taught how to remove it.

When crippled by fear, it doesn't matter whether or not the danger is real. In 90% of cases the fear isn't real but an illusion. Sometimes you are so paralyzed by fear that you can't move. Have you ever experienced that?

You're afraid to move a hand, to take a step or look out from under the blanket. You're afraid of the future. Fear is disarming. When you are afraid, you can't move, because your thoughts, emotions, will and even body are bound. You are paralyzed by fear. When a person is paralyzed, it means that some parts of their body don't work or follow instructions from the brain. You'd think it would be easy just to get up and walk, but because of fear, there is no connection between the brain and the body. That's how demonic fear paralyzes and makes someone unable to do anything, or to follow God's instructions."

"I've experienced that. I'm usually scared when my husband or child is out late. I can't do anything if I don't hear from them. I can't even call anyone," Vera stated.

"Then there are anxiety, worries, and obsessive thoughts," Rita explained. "Your husband is working late or his phone is out of calling range, and you already have started thinking thoughts like, 'Maybe he had an accident, or he was beaten up by someone, or arrested by the police.' And you are already in a state of anxiety and fear, in the grip of concern. Terrible pictures spin in your head, and it's more and more difficult to stop them. When your husband comes home you're all wound up and shaking, when in fact, his phone had just died, or he had just been chatting with a friend. That's how the devil involves people in his game.

In such cases, I usually do the opposite. I make the phone ring off the hook and sound an alarm.

Girls, I think I've just figured out why I have not divorced yet. I'm scared. I'm afraid to be alone. But that's wrong. That's the wrong reason for preserving the family, right?

It's very important for us to not be guided by fear in our lives. Fear is the worst reason for any action.

'**Do not be afraid**; only **believe**, and she will be made well.' (Luke 8:50) Jesus said this to the ruler of the synagogue when He was told that his daughter had died. If Jesus asked him not to be afraid, then fear could interfere with solving a problem. Fear is one of the strongest weapons of Satan. The devil lies and frightens, dragging a person into slavery. The devil tries to intimidate and deceive us, whispering that he is done with our family and even Jesus can't help. But IT'S A LIE. Jesus can always help, no matter how complicated the situation is.

Job said, 'For the thing I greatly feared has come upon me.' If we don't deal with fear, it will deal with us and bring into our lives what we've greatly feared. The demons are attracted by the 'smell' of fear like dogs who attack those who fear them.

Fear is also faith, but it's of the devil. It is faith in the power of the devil to do something in your life or the lives of your loved ones. When we are afraid, we give Satan the power to do something. But, when we aren't afraid, it shows that we believe in the power of God, in the power of the Lord, to do something beautiful and wonderful. It shows that we believe that God is able to save our husbands. Thus, by our faith, we give God the power to do something in our lives.

Jesus says, 'Do not be afraid!' This means to not let the devil deceive you, as if he had the right to do something in the life of your husband without God's knowledge. God knows everything, sees everything, and is able to do everything. A single hair doesn't fall off your head without His knowledge.

We need to let God save us from fear. God gives us the power to conquer any fear. This power is His love and faith! When we are not afraid, we can do anything.

For God has not given us a spirit of fear, but of power and of love and of a sound mind.

∾ 2 Timothy 1:7

Be filled with His love and strengthened in His power. God strengthens us and gives us wisdom to do the right things. Our actions shouldn't be based on fear. Our actions must be based on His love, power and prudence.

There is no fear in love; but perfect love casts out fear...   1 John 4:18

God has perfect love. When we accept it, it casts out fear from our lives. The more love we receive from God, the more confident we become.

In order to get free from an addiction, you will have to be courageous, prudent and keep calm. How to be courageous and to not be afraid? How to act wisely? The answer is in the Book of Joshua.

Be strong and of good courage, for to this people you shall divide as an inheritance the land which I swore to their fathers to give them. Only be strong and very courageous, that you may observe to do according to all the law which Moses My servant commanded you; do not turn from it to the right hand or to the left, that you may prosper wherever you go. This Book of the Law shall not depart from your mouth, but you shall meditate in it day and night, that you may observe to do according to all that is written in it. For then you will make your way prosperous, and then you will have good success. Have I not commanded you? Be strong and of good courage; do not be afraid, nor be dismayed, for the Lord your God is with you wherever you go.   ∽ Joshua 1:6–9

Do not be afraid, because God is with you wherever you go. You have to be aware of it, meditate on it, read it over and over, and believe! To do what is right, God commands us to meditate on His Word, to proclaim the truth and to act as written in the Word of God. Then God will give you wisdom for everything you do. You will understand how and when you should act.

DO NOT BE AFRAID; only BELIEVE, and she will be made well.   ∽ Luke 8:50

Only believe! Believe the Lord, because there is nothing impossible for Him!

Now faith is the substance of things hoped for, the evidence of things not seen.

∽ Hebrews 11:1

We believe that some things exist, although we don't see them.

Similarly, we need to believe that our husband will be free, although this is not yet visible. This freedom already exists in the spiritual world, because Jesus acquired it more than 2,000 years ago. Our faith has the power to bring what we need and what is rightfully ours from the spiritual world into the physical one.

> But without faith it is impossible to please Him,
> for he who comes to God must believe that He
> is, and that He is a rewarder of those who dili-
> gently seek Him.    Hebrews 11:6

It is important for God that we believe in Him. If you want to receive something from God, you need to desperately believe in Him, trust Him and just know that He will help, support and give what you ask Him for.

If you want to impress God (if, of course, you can say so), believe Him no matter what. Sincere faith is so pleasing to God that He will give you everything you ask of Him.

Trust Him like a small child trusts their parents. Don't doubt Him, His love for you, His desire to help you and His ability to save your husband.

Don't be afraid, believe God, and your family will be saved! Your husband will be the head! Your children will have a good and loving dad."

CHAPTER 7

Ruined Holiday

Lorena didn't come to the group after vacation. She couldn't escape from the city during the summer, because she had a lot of work. She was tired, and it already seemed that she would break down and explode. Once again, Lorena found her husband at home in a state of extreme narcotic intoxication, and she had to call an ambulance to bring him to life. It was just a short step to overdose.

After all treatments, Lorena went into the kitchen to talk with the doctor and hand him the money for the work.

"Lady, you are young and beautiful," the doctor began, "Why do you tolerate it? Understand, there are no former drug addicts."

"Doctor, he's my husband."

"Yes, I understand you. No one wants to be alone. But, believe me, you've got your whole life ahead of you. And he will ruin it."

"Thank you, doctor, for your advice. We'll figure it out on our own," Lorena responded rudely.

When the ambulance left, Lorena began to talk to herself, without even noticing it, saying, "I'm strong! I can handle it! I'll get him out. I'm not going to abandon him. I don't believe that there is no way out of this trouble.

This monster — drugs — will not take my husband away from me. If he had cancer, I wouldn't divorce him, but fight for him. And if he had an accident, I would care for him. So why should I give up and give him over to alcohol and drugs? No, it's not happening.

I'm strong! I can do it! I'll prove that there is a way out.

After all, we are a family, and we love each other. So everybody has turned their backs on us, big deal! It means they aren't our friends at all. It's okay! We can handle this. We've been through worse.

I've made up my mind. We need to go on vacation. Far from his friends and temptations, things will get better.

Done! We'll pack a suitcase and it will be a new start for us. Sun, sea, change of scenery and no worries! What better way to change everything once and for all.

I need to talk to my mom to leave the children with her."

Lorena began to translate her thoughts into reality. First of all, she called the travel agency and bought a tour. Then she dealt with the work issues and took the children to her mother. She packed a suitcase and was full of hope for the future. She couldn't even guess that her darling had very different plans for that vacation.

He only wanted to hold out one day and night and hide the drugs so that his wife didn't guess. His purpose for the trip was totally different.

"We aren't going abroad," her husband said. "Suit yourself, but I won't go by plane."

Despite her usual impatience for resisting her plans, Lorena agreed. She simply didn't have the strength to argue with him.

She returned the tour package.

"Okay, we'll have a vacation in our country," Lorena thought. "It's no big deal. Very patriotic and practical. Indeed, why do we have to fly somewhere if we haven't seen our own country yet? To be honest, I don't care. I would even go to the village, if only my husband was free."

It was only later that she realized that her husband couldn't take drugs abroad. And even if he could, it was unreasonably risky.

Lorena and her husband arrived at the vacation destination and unpacked their belongings. Everything seemed to start well.

"Where are my nasal drops? What did you do with them?" he asked.

"I don't know. I don't watch over your drops." Lorena replied.

"You did that on purpose! Don't you understand that I've been using them for 10 years? I can't breathe out of my nose without them. Did you come here to mock me?" he questioned.

"I didn't take your drops!" Lorena retorted. "You'll have to tell that to someone else! I'm sick of you! I'm not going to dance to your tune! I'm not a lapdog to you! Leave me alone!"

"Oh, screw you! I'm fed up with all this!" he exclaimed angrily.

Slamming the door, he left. Where did he go? Why?

Several hours passed. "What a good start of vacation!" Lorena thought. "It's probably my fault. Why do I provoke him? I knew that he could be aggressive. Maybe I wasn't attentive to him. Maybe I didn't have to be so tough with him. Probably, I should be more understanding. Maybe ... Probably ... I should ... I shouldn't... You never know for sure how to act. These pangs and doubts are simply eating me alive. Yes, for sure, it's my fault. I should be..," Lorena suddenly stopped thinking and recalled what Rita had said at the fellowship group:

"If you constantly **feel guilty and have doubts**, they prevent you from coming to your senses and becoming sober.

By guilt, we can manipulate a person, pull their strings and they will do what we want. The devil is the accuser and slanderer. He will blame you, saying that it's your fault; that you did something wrong, that you didn't behave in proper way.

Husbands blame their wives for bugging them, behaving badly, not understanding them and attribute their drinking to all of this.

It must be understood that a wife isn't perfect, but this doesn't allow her husband to be unruly, get drunk, fight or take drugs.

Guilt arises from an inability to help. You begin to feel guilty because you can't help him. You do your best, but it doesn't work. And then you suddenly start thinking, 'Maybe I didn't try hard enough. Maybe I could've done something else.'

The main reason for guilt is a misperception that a wife is responsible for her husband's addiction. That's not true. It's a lie. The wife doesn't bear any responsibility for that. The devil as the father of lies constantly tries to make a person feel guilty, useless and worthless.

If you start to believe him that you are guilty of your husband's unwillingness to quit drinking or taking drugs, you will have **a sense of guilt**. And **if you are guilty, you deserve punishment. That's why** you tolerate a wrong attitude toward yourself. At the same time, you may think, 'It's my fault! I deserved it.'

The devil will lie that you don't deserve a different life. But it's a lie in order to not let you escape slavery. You can't be responsible for another person. The husband is an adult and a person."

Lorena also recalled how Rita told a story from her life:

"My husband suffered a psychotic breakdown and wasn't himself for several days. It was a real spiritual oppression.

The first thing he did was blame me. Looking into my eyes, he said,

'Repent, it's your fault.'

'Why?' I asked.

'You know,' he answered.

'I don't know,' I objected.

'Everyone knows, and the pastor knows. Repent, it's all because of you.'

I couldn't understand what was happening and started to search my thoughts and emotions, because I wanted to understand what to repent for. Then I realized that it wasn't my husband's voice. It was Satan, accusing me. He wanted to slander me, to cut the ground from under my feet and to make me feel guilty, so that I'd feel bad and unworthy. Why did he do that? So that I couldn't come to the throne of God's grace and mercy with boldness and ask God for healing and freedom for myself and my husband.

Guilt doesn't allow us to raise our heads to heaven, because if we feel we don't deserve something, how can we ask God for it?

But, in fact, it's not like that! We can come to God without fear and shame because we are His children. Jesus took all the blame upon himself, so we are not guilty anymore."

"It's all clear now!" exclaimed Lorena. "I'm not guilty. The devil wants to deceive me. It won't work! I'm going to continue fighting."

Suddenly she thought, "Where are his drops? He always has 3 bottles in each pocket." Lorena checked the first aid kit and found the drops. "Here are the drops. Also he is likely to have another bottle in his pocket. I'm beginning to understand that it was only an excuse to be out of my sight. It was so clear. And why do I always get fooled by the same tricks? I shouldn't have shouted at him, but searched for the drops at once."

Lorena went looking for her husband. She went to every bar in the area, but didn't find him. In the meantime, it got dark and a little scary. There were drunken men and a lot of cigarette smoke around. Near the bar, a fight was just getting started. "And this is called vacation! Next time we will go to a nicer place; maybe, somewhere abroad. This is not what I've been working hard for all year!"

She returned home. Her husband was already there, and as the saying goes, there was peace and quiet. His was in a good mood.

"Did you take a walk? Let's go out for dinner. I found a good restaurant here," the husband blurted out from the doorway.

"Lord, this is truly the theatre of the absurd! What's going on?" Lorena thought.

"It is clear that he took a dose, and now he is relaxed. And I'm so naïve to believe that we've come here to change our lives."

During that vacation Lorena learned how to not scream and quarrel.

Always, when her husband needed to run away from home for drugs on a day off and whenever he just couldn't leave, he provoked her into a scandal. And in the middle of the scandal, always slamming the door, her husband just left, making her feel guilty for his leaving and taking drugs.

But step by step, God began to change it. She stopped responding to the provocations. Then it was almost impossible to drive Lorena out of peace. She didn't shout, but spoke calmly and with understanding. That behavior blew her husband's mind. He simply didn't know what to do because he couldn't blame her and run away, slamming the door. That kind of reaction spoilt his long-standing scenario.

CHAPTER 8

Take Out the Garbage

"Girls, we're going to take out the garbage today," Rita said, announcing the topic of the group.

"Oh, cool! But my husband takes out the garbage. We share our duties in this way. Although, he sometimes forgets to do it. But I deliberately wait for him to do what he has to, even if the garbage smell spreads throughout the whole apartment," Alla told a marvelous story.

"Oh, Alla! If I waited for my husband to take out the garbage, then the neighbors would rather voluntarily decide to help me rather than wait for him to do it, because you'll never get any help of out him."

"Here we go! Before I can announce the topic, everyone has already started a discussion and murmuring," Rita said with a smile. "Let me begin please. Otherwise you'll be thinking about what I meant till the next group."

"Sorry, Rita," Alla said. "It's just a burning issue. It's not so hard to take out the garbage, but it's annoying that my husband doesn't even want to do little things."

"Well, I'm glad you've gotten excited about the topic. I see that everyone agrees that it is necessary to take out the garbage from the house. Because if it isn't taken out for a long time, everyone will smell it.

But the most important thing isn't taking out the garbage that is in the bin, but the garbage that is in the heart.

The Bible says:

> Keep your heart with all diligence, for out of it spring the issues of life.   ❧ Proverbs 4:23

All issues spring out of our heart, because how a person lives originates from their heart. If there are grievances, unforgiveness, anger and worry in the heart, it's hard for a person to live in such an atmosphere, and the smell is very bad. Therefore, all dirt and garbage must be taken out of your heart.

Often we are mistaken. What is bad and dirty we mask and hide in the heart. We try to make it so nobody finds out and notices that we have it.

We show to people only those things which, in our opinion, are good, in order to show that we are doing well.

For example, at home we quarrel with our husbands, but when we come to church, we take their arms, so that nobody thinks that there is something wrong in our families. Then we return home and quarrel again. And it can last for years.

It's like we pull garbage into the house, but take out everything good. As a result, a garbage dump is formed at home where we live, and everything good is taken out of the house. And there is emptiness in the heart.

Therefore, we constantly suffer from stress and worry about how to conceal and disguise the reality from people. We get tired of this and nothing changes for the better. But you can spend your energy not on trying to seem happy and cheerful, but on becoming so.

None of you is going to argue that in speaking about the house, we need to remove the dirt, and bring in new and good things. But when it comes to the heart, you need to work on yourself to do the same."

Judging

Rita continued, "The first thing you need to get rid of is judging others. At first glance, it may seem that this is a harmless thing, and we let it lie somewhere. So we talked to a friend and judged someone together. Big deal. But, in fact, judgment is a sneaky enemy and very dangerous for life.

> Therefore you are inexcusable, O man, whoever you are who judges, for in whatever you judge another you condemn yourself; for you who judge practice the same things.
>
>   ❧ Romans 2:1

The one who judges, practices the same things. I noticed that everything I judged came into my life after a while.

I didn't understand how one could marry a drug addict, and after a while I faced the same situation. For me, the wives of drug addicts were strange and didn't command any respect. My thoughts were, 'How can that person allow someone to treat her like that? She needs to respect herself. Probably, they are not quite right in the head,' I thought. But when I found myself in the same trap, I began to understand that those women were poor and in trouble. I judged women who didn't divorce drunkards, and after a time I experienced how difficult it was.

A person who judges the actions of another person or a group of people today, will find themselves in the same situation after a while.

Women who had judged their friends for treason were tempted to commit adultery. Daughters who had judged their mothers for tolerating the boorish attitude of their fathers started families with men who had the same attitude towards them, and they couldn't escape that.

Parents who had judged other parents whose children drank or smoked, were faced with the fact that their children, when becoming older, fell for the same things.

People who had quit doing drugs or alcohol judged those who couldn't quit, and after a while they got into that trouble again. And the angrier a person who judges is, the more difficult the situations and troubles they have in life.

Judging is like a boomerang, and God warns about it in the Word of God. It really works. It's the devil's trap to make something bad happen in our lives.

Often we judge someone because we simply don't know how difficult it is for a person and what they go through. We take the place of a judge and pass sentences, because we believe that a person deserves punishment. But by doing this, we pass sentence on ourselves.

God doesn't give us the right to judge people. Only He is the Righteous Judge. God Himself doesn't hurry to judge, because His mercy is above judgment. He is gracious, understanding and loving. And we can't neglect His kindness.

It is better to try to understand why a person does something, than to judge them. It is necessary to repent before God for those situations where we have judged people, so that our heart is purified and this seed of judgment doesn't become effective in our life.

> Therefore you are inexcusable, O man, whoever you are who judge, for in whatever you judge another you condemn yourself; for you who judge practice the same things. But we know that the judgment of God is according to truth against those who practice such things. And do you think this, O man, you who judge those practicing such things, and doing the same, that you will escape the judgment of God? Or do you despise the riches of His goodness, forbearance, and longsuffering, not knowing that the goodness of God leads you to repentance?
>
> ⤎ Romans 2:1-4

God's goodness leads us to repentance. It is necessary to repent for every judgment. Remember, maybe you judged women who married addicts, or those who tolerated something, or those who couldn't get free from addiction."

"Rita, I judged my husband for being weak and unable to give up drugs," Lorena said.

"When you judge your husband, you harm both yourself and your husband. In judging someone, we throw a stone at them, and this stone strikes a painful blow. This doesn't give someone the strength to sin no more, but only causes unbearable pain, and it gets harder and harder for a person to get free. Under the pressure of condemnation, it is difficult for a person to rise up. A person feels incomplete, dirty and unworthy. They lose their faith that they will be able to sin no more and quit drugs or alcohol. God is rich in grace and mercy. God is long-suffering. His grace leads to repentance, and therefore, to changes in life. His grace gives strength to rise and to sin no more.

Once a woman caught in the sin of adultery was brought to Jesus.

Jesus was the only One who had the right to condemn her, because among all, He alone was without sin.

But He didn't do it, because condemnation wouldn't give the power to that woman to rise up, be free and live a new life.

> Then the scribes and Pharisees brought to Him a woman caught in adultery. And when they had set her in the midst, they said to Him, "Teacher, this woman was caught in adultery, in the very act. Now Moses, in the law, commanded us that such should be stoned. But what do You say?" This they said, testing Him, that they might have something of which to accuse Him. But Jesus stooped down and wrote on the ground with His finger, as though He didn't hear. So when they continued asking Him, He raised Himself up and said to them, "He who is without sin among you, let him throw a stone at her first." And again He stooped down and wrote on the ground. Then those who heard it, being convicted by their conscience, went out one by one, beginning

with the oldest even to the last. And Jesus was left alone, and the woman standing in the midst. When Jesus had raised Himself up and saw no one but the woman, He said to her, "Woman, where are those accusers of yours? Has no one condemned you?" She said, "No one, Lord." And Jesus said to her, "Neither do I condemn you; go and sin no more."

ھ John 8:3–11

We need to learn from Jesus to be merciful to people. This will help us to not get into different troubles and help people, who are near us, to rise up."

"I realized that every time I judged my husband, I didn't help him to solve the problem, but it got worse. Lord, please help me to not act in such a way!" Lorena said.

Anger and Rage

"You also need to take out anger and rage. They will prevent you from moving towards victory. I want to tell you a story from my life," Rita continued.

"Almost every day I quarreled with my husband, because he couldn't solve the problem of his addiction. What bothered me the most was that he lied. His lies drove me crazy. I was ready to strangle him. I simply couldn't cope with my emotions. I broke dishes, screamed at children, children cried, but nothing changed. That evening my husband came in, in a state of extreme drug intoxication. What irritated me the most was that he didn't admit it. He always insisted that he was sober and had been using nothing for a long time. I couldn't force the truth out of him, although it was so clear. At that moment, during the scandal, I had a knife at hand. I grabbed that knife and put it to his throat. My anger was so strong that I could murder him, and I had as much strength as men did. My husband was frightened.

I believe that God saved me with his invisible hand and didn't allow the terrible thing to happen. I fell to the floor and dropped the knife. My hands were shaking, and I was terribly scared. 'Oh, God, I could have killed a man! I could have killed my husband!' I never thought that something like that could happen to me. I never thought that an ordinary person could become a murderer. I didn't control myself. I was very scared. 'What am I reduced to? I'm no better than him. He is addicted to drugs, and I'm obsessed with anger. It's just insane. It's scary to be near me.' Of course, that event sobered my husband up, but it sobered me more. I began to pray and ask God to set me free. I sincerely asked God to change ME, not him.'"

"It's like you're talking about me. I also can't help it. I'm ashamed to admit it, but in an instant I can turn into a crazy drama queen, and thereafter I'm shaking and just can't calm down," Alla said.

"The anger didn't go away right afterwards, but every time it started to rise up, I quickly went into the bathroom, locked the door and asked God to help me, or I got dressed and went for a walk to talk to God and pray in tongues. All your anger is better to bring down on the devil, because, in fact, it's he who is guilty of all this. In prayer, command Satan to let your husband go and to get out. But always talk to God, because it's He Who gives us strength. When God's peace came again, I returned home."

Weariness and oppression

"The devil always wants to get us in a state of oppression. In this state, you don't see the way out or even a hint of change. You lose heart and don't see the point in doing anything. You don't see the point in fighting. Satan wants you to surrender and always be in sorrow.

I was in such a state. I was so depressed that I didn't see the point in anything. I didn't want to take care of myself. I didn't want to put on make-up, dress with care or do my hair. I saw no point in all of that. I didn't want to clean the apartment and cook. In general, I didn't want to do anything. My life had no meaning anymore.

The oppressor wants to break you inside and enslave your will. He makes you dance to his tune. His task is to suppress you, to make you incapable of doing anything and to destroy your dreams and desires. He infringes on your rights and limits your freedom, as well as your ability to create, live and develop.

Under the influence of oppression, it is impossible to win. An oppressed person can't do anything. When I was oppressed, I couldn't pray and praise God, make decisions, or break through spiritually.

It was as if someone wanted to put me in a bed under a blanket so I would huddle up in a corner, feel sorry for myself and not come out. You don't see the point in getting up in the morning. Sometimes, because of being tired or depressed, you hide out in sleeping. Even the disciples of Jesus fell asleep under the weight of oppression, when Jesus asked them to stay awake and pray.

> When He rose up from prayer, and had come to His disciples, He found them sleeping from sorrow.
>
> ◦◦ Luke 22:45

Sorrow, sadness and weariness exhaust a person. Another translation says that the disciples slept because they were **exhausted** by sadness.

I started to get sick due to nervous tension and constant depression. I constantly felt faint, had a fever and inflammation in my body. Doctors couldn't understand what was going on. The human body doesn't handle oppressive weariness.

In the Bible it is written that a broken spirit dries the bones, and I felt it.

> A merry heart does good, like medicine, but a broken spirit dries the bones.
>
> ◦◦ Proverbs 17:22

I finally realized what was happening to me. The unclean spirits of oppression and weariness were attacking me, and I decided to resist them. Therefore, every time I got a wave of oppression or weariness, I asked God for help.

> Now therefore, behold, the cry of the children of Israel has come to Me, and I have also seen the oppression with which the Egyptians oppress them.
>
> ◦◦ Exodus 3:9

God hears our cries for help. He sees those who oppress us and delivers us from slavery.

I turned on worship music and tried to rejoice. With the first few songs it was hard, but then my spirit came alive and I felt real joy and confidence in the future. I prayed in tongues and specifically commanded those spirits to be gone in the name of Jesus. They were gone, but after a while came back again. Sometimes I had to confront them almost every hour, but each time less and less frequently. The less I wanted to attend our fellowship group or church prayer meeting, the earlier I went there, in order to not change my mind. I deliberately didn't come home after work, even if I had time, because I knew that it would be more difficult to leave the house, and I could have a blind spot.

It was a battle for my freedom — freedom to praise God, freedom to serve Him, freedom to rejoice and live.

Don't be tolerant of your enemy. You won't be able to win if you tolerate what you don't have to. Oppression and weariness are evil enemies directed by the devil to destroy your personality and your body. These are traps that prevent you from getting victory in your life.

Jesus gives us victory. He gives joy for tears, garments of glory for desperation and comfort for sorrow. He heals the heart that has been broken by the circumstances of life. God wants to show His glory through us.

> "The Spirit of the Lord God is upon Me, Because the Lord has anointed Me To preach good tidings to the poor; He has sent Me to heal the brokenhearted, To proclaim liberty to the captives, And the opening of the prison to those who are bound; to proclaim the acceptable year of the Lord, and the day of vengeance of our God; to

comfort all who mourn, to console those who mourn in Zion, to give them beauty for ashes, the oil of joy for mourning, the garment of praise for the spirit of heaviness; that they may be called trees of righteousness, the planting of the Lord, that He may be glorified."

ɷ Isaiah 61:1–3

If you are depressed, you are already trapped. If you are discouraged, you won't win. Get rid of oppression and the power of God will manifest!

God wants our joy to be based on Him and not on earthly circumstances. It is necessary to learn to rejoice no matter what.

Anxiety and worry attract a dull spirit to us. That's why we need God's peace. In His hands we are safe.

Do what the ruler of the synagogue Jairus did. His daughter was lying down and at the point of death, but he found the strength to leave home to find a solution. He could sit next to his dying daughter and with tears in his eyes hold her hand, realizing that those were the last hours of her life. But he decided to get out of that atmosphere of disease, threat and fear of the near-death condition of the family member. Everyone at his home was infected by that atmosphere. It is impossible to be in a state of depression, fear and threat and at the same time bring healing, victory and life to another person. A person can't give what they don't have. What does it mean to get out of the atmosphere of oppression? It means that you know and understand what is happening in your home, but believe that there is a way out of this situation. It means that your mood, emotions and decisions no longer depend on what is happening, but on what is said in the Word of God.

It means that you leave this state and go to find Jesus to invite Him into your home. It means that you learn to find God in prayer, in the Bible, and you go to meetings of believers. Jesus will never refuse to come to your house and solve your problem. Come out of oppression and rejoice! Your victory is coming soon!"

Resentment and unforgiveness

Continuing on, Rita explained, "Probably the most difficult thing for a woman is to forgive someone for breaking her dreams of family happiness.

Failed hopes are like betrayal. It's like someone deprives you of the most precious thing that you have. It's as if your husband has betrayed you and chosen drugs. Every time, abusing your trust, he betrays again and again. You say, 'I can't forgive him for breaking my dreams and depriving me of my desires. I expected that I would be a princess in a white dress, but was back at the bottom of the ladder.' It's difficult to forgive even myself for making such a choice, which has caused a complete ruining of my dream of family happiness.

In order for your life to become new, you need to forgive your husband for all the things he has done and for the pain he has caused.

You need to forgive your husband and his friends. You know and have memories of those who've caused you to suffer.

When we forgive, we let go of the past. Forgive those things which were tied to you and have hurt you. Do we really need something disgusting and unpleasant to be tied to us?"

"I have heard that there used to be such an execution. A corpse was tied to the back of a living person. The corpse decomposed and was eaten by worms. And when worms were done with the corpse, they began to eat the living body," Lorena chided.

"Ugh, Lorena! You have nothing more to talk about! That's disgusting!" Alla cried.

"Yes, it's terrible. But, frankly, that's how unforgiveness works. The sooner you throw it off your back and cleanse yourself, the faster you'll be in perfect condition," Rita said.

"We have to forgive as soon as possible. In such a way you get rid of everything bad and don't tie yourself to anything disgusting. The longer you feel offended, the deeper the resentment penetrates your heart and destroys you from within. Resentment and unforgiveness don't do you any good. They block your breakthrough for those things you ask God for. God commands us to forgive when we come to Him in prayer, so that there are no obstacles in getting an answer.

Especially God says:

> Therefore I say to you, whatever things you ask when you pray, believe that you receive them, and you will have them. "And whenever you stand praying, if you have anything against anyone, forgive him, that your Father in heaven may also forgive you your trespasses. But if you do not forgive, neither will your Father in heaven forgive your trespasses." ⁓ Mark 11:24–26

Once I tried to resent my husband again, but at that time I didn't know that God had already given me the gift to forget resentments. I remembered that I resented him, but I couldn't remember for what. My husband asked me why I was offended, I couldn't respond and just started laughing."

"Rita, it's because you resented him for something little. But it's hard to forgive for something serious," said Lorena.

"Start practicing. Forgiveness is your decision. You simply have to decide to forgive your husband for the things he's done. After all, God forgives us. I know that your husbands have done you wrong, betrayed and hurt you. We have also behaved badly toward God and people, but He forgives us and expects that we forgive too. God treats us according to His grace and not according to what we deserve. We deserve punishment, but He has mercy on us. Treat your husbands not according to what they deserve, but by grace. And you will see how God's mercy begins to flow into your life."

CHAPTER 9

Mentor

L orena and Alla were gone for a month, then showed up again at the fellowship group. Everyone was happy about their return.

"And where were you? You missed so many meetings! I called you and you promised to come, but didn't," Vera asked.

"We're going to tell you. In general, we were in many places. First, we visited a kind of 'Encounter', where we were told that there we would be able to get rid of everything bad in our lives so that no curse could follow us," Lorena began.

"Well, we participated in this," Alla summed up.

"Then we were invited to the ministry of freedom. We decided that it was high time to do something, because there was no progress in our lives."

"Then we visited a rehabilitation center to send Lorena's husband there," said Alla.

"And what?" asked Vera.

"Nothing. They said that I had to kick him out of the house, take his money and change the door lock," Lorena said.

"Yes, but in another place they said that I had to treat him with love; that is, to wash his feet, cook for him and just melt his heart with love," Alla said. "In one place they said that it was a spiritual curse, and in another that he simply didn't want to quit. In short, Rita, I'm so confused. Now I don't know what to do- to kick him out or not. And they also frightened me with talk about those curses."

"Ok, travelers, let's talk," declared Rita, "A person doesn't need to be treated for a disease by several different doctors. Let's imagine that a person had a disease, and they decided to go to five different doctors and be treated according to five different programs. And all of the doctors didn't know anything about the decision of their patient. Surely, that person would have serious problems, because the medications prescribed by different doctors might be incompatible, as well as the information and the diagnoses would be different. In such a case, all those doctors wouldn't understand what was happening to the person, and why their treatments didn't help. Each of the doctors had prescribed treatment with a certain medication and was watching how that medication was received by the patient's body because that was needed to decide whether to change it or to increase the dose. But they wouldn't have an adequate picture of the patient's health, because at the same time the patient took other medicines which were prescribed by other doctors, and all the doctors didn't know anything about that situation. Moreover, everything was complicated by the fact that there were not just two doctors, but five... And in addition to all that, the patient decided to try the folk medicine following the grandmother's recipes. So it turned out that the treatment was not effective, because there was no specific treatment program and one professional."

"Rita, I never thought like that," Lorena stated, "I thought that the more places I would visit and the more things I would do, the better."

"Lorena, you have tried this method. What is the result?"

"To be honest Rita, I don't understand anything at all. I was only running back and forth. I don't understand what is right. How to pray? How to fast? Where to go — to doctors or rehabilitation centers? Or just to divorce? I'm confused, and now there's such a mess is in my head."

"Of course, Lorena! You just have indigestion. You know, like in the case of improper nutrition."

"Oh, what you are saying is so true!" Lorena agreed.

"You know, if you put it all together — Japanese sushi, Russian salad, dresser herring salad and milk, and ate, you can only imagine how you would feel after that. That wouldn't be useful to you. Especially if you did it more than once and every day." said Rita.

"Yes, that's for sure." declared Lorena.

"Each person has an earthly family, and the church is also a family. You need to decide what church is going to be your family and the place where you eat. Then you won't be confused. After all, when everything goes in one direction, the food is balanced. Just as at home the mother cooks for everyone in the family, so in the church everyone eats spiritual food.

Let me give you another example. If you have a summer house or you live in a village, it will be easy for you to imagine a vegetable garden. Imagine that you had a fifteen acre plot for gardening. Of course it was intended to bring some sort of harvest, so you wanted to grow something there. Spring came, and your aunt went to your garden and planted parsley and dill. After a while, your uncle came, and in the same place where your aunt planted the green vegetables, he planted potatoes. The next day, your parents, having no idea about the seeds which had already been planted in the garden, decided to plant strawberries there. And finally someone else came and planted flowers and grass. Just think what kind of harvest would it be? It is unlikely that you, as the landlady, expected this kind of harvest. And what if every one of your relatives started to fertilize it all? Please note that all the people had good intentions and planted good seeds, but the result was still bad. If only one person was in charge of the vegetable garden, they would've prepared the beds, planted every vegetable in due time and place, and properly fertilized it. As a result, there would be a completely different HARVEST!

Our hearts are like gardens, where a good landlord sows seeds to obtain a result. He knows at what time it is necessary to pull weeds and when it is too early. He knows what has to be done. But we prepare our hearts and decide whether to allow someone to plant there or not."

"Well, not all of us are landladies, but all of us are beauties," Rita continued, smiling. "That's the way I see it.

It's like a woman who wore clothes of different styles: a fur hat, an evening dress, sneakers and a sports sweatshirt. It's like someone who decided that she would wear an evening dress and didn't know that it was supposed to be a sporty look.

When your "wardrobe" is prepared for an event by one pastor, he does everything consistently and in due time, and that's why he is not going to make you wear sneakers and heels at the same time. But if you run from church to church, the situation will be the following. One pastor gives you an evening dress today (because he is preparing the church for ball), and is going to give you shoes tomorrow. But tomorrow you won't be here, because you will go to another church, where you should wear sneakers. And the sneakers are right for that second church, because yesterday they wore a sports suit, since they planned to go in for sports.

Everything goes well when it is harmonious and balanced.

I recently had the opportunity to get acquainted with a woman who had been visiting different places to solve her problem for many years. Her mind, her way of thinking and life were like that garden, in which different kinds of seeds were planted. She was so confused about everything. So don't experiment with your life, because you only live once. Don't let just anyone sow seeds in your heart. Jesus compares our hearts to soil, and your results depend on who you allow to sow seeds there. And also it is very important what kind of soil it is and whether it is ready to take the seeds."

"Rita, does that mean that we can't watch any other services and read books by other authors?"

"Of course, you can. The main thing though is to read the Bible. It is very important to be dedicated to your church and your pastor in order to hear his voice and have a proper understanding of everything. By the way, various preachers are often invited to the church, so the point isn't that you can't do that. When God leads you and you know the path your family follows, you have spiritual discernment. You will understand what kind of food you need, what is good, and what is dangerous. So you not only can, but also have to read books and watch sermons of other pastors. I mean, if you don't know much yet, you should consult your mentor.

It is sad to look at people who run from church to church, from ministry to ministry, from one doctor to another, without following what they are taught and told. They seem to expect that suddenly someone will touch them with some kind of magic wand or say the right words and the problem will be solved. But that's a lie. It's good for the devil if a person doesn't have roots, because they will have no fruit. Try to transplant a tree in new soil every day and see what will happen to it, even if the soil is always good. Eventually it will wither and have no fruit. So why do we think that if we constantly transplant ourselves into different soils, it will work out? It is necessary to make a decision and choose a church, ministry, fellowship group and mentor who will help you and teach you.

Appropriate communication is also very important.

Tell me who your friends are and I will tell you who you are or will be. This is true, no matter how much effort we make on the way to our freedom. If we don't change our circle of friends we will return to old things. Having quit drugs, a person shouldn't communicate with old friends who are still addicts because this person will fall into this slavery again.

Many people go to their friends to tell them that there is a way out of the bondage of drug and alcohol addiction. But it is a mistake to go to your friends to tell them this when you've just gotten free. This is how a lot of people become addicted again."

"I've been telling my husband for a long time not to communicate with his friends. They won't do you any good," Lorena said.

"Lorena, this also applies to wives," Rita explained, "Often the wife thinks that her husband has to change friends, because he has problems, but she can continue her former way of life, to hang out with unbelievers who smoke, go to nightclubs and drink wine and champagne. She thinks that it's normal to keep company with negative relatives and keep on drinking, and at the same time she forbids her husband to drink. She thinks, 'Let him see how others drink and don't get drunk.' The wife doesn't understand what her husband is feeling and doesn't realize that in the spiritual world she is defeated in the fight for her family. The addiction is a shared problem, so everybody has to change.

Believe me, these changes are worth it. There is nothing better than life with God. The happiest people earth are those who believe in Jesus Christ and live by His Word of Life."

CHAPTER 10

Temptation to Sin

Lorena's husband went to their summer house for a week. The doorbell rang. Lorena was surprised, thinking, "Who could that be?" Maybe someone her husband owed money to? But who could know that she didn't go to work today?

Lorena opened the door and couldn't believe her eyes. How could that be? Why? How? A lot of thoughts flew in her head in a second.

Leonid was standing with flowers at the door. Leonid was Lorena's first love. They quarreled because of some trifles and broke up. All of the old feelings came up.

"Can I come in?" Leonid asked.

"Why?" Lorena asked.

"We're not enemies, Lorena. May I have some tea, please?"

Lorena let him in.

"My husband might come, and I don't think he'll be pleased with your visiting."

"We aren't doing anything wrong," Leonid said.

Leonid looked wonderful. His body was pumped up from working out and tanned, and he seemed to have specially dressed so that his clothes emphasized his muscles.

They sat, talked and recalled their youth, mutual acquaintances, their company and various interesting moments of life.

Lorena, looking at Leonid, felt a strong excitement. She had not had an intimate relationship with her husband for a long time, and frankly, she didn't want to. The sight of her husband in a state of drug intoxication disgusted her. So her female need for affection wasn't satisfied.

Leonid, feeling that the "victim" was ready, started to act decisively.

Lorena found the strength to resist and asked Leonid to leave.

"To be honest," she told Rita, "a little more and I wouldn't have been able to resist. I don't understand how he knew. What a coincidence!

You know, I started to think, 'For what purpose do I turn down a new relationship, because there are men who aren't drug addicts, who are handsome and successful? Why am I going through all this?"

"For the devil, this isn't a new trick," Rita replied. "He used it always, from the time of the Garden of Eden, when he seduced a woman to eat the forbidden fruit.

> So when the woman saw that the tree was good for food, that it was pleasant to the eyes, and a tree desirable to make one wise, she took of its fruit and ate. She also gave to her husband with her, and he ate.   ∽ Genesis 3:6

That tree was always in the Garden, and for sure, Eve walked past it more than once. But that time she looked at it as a food source, thought of its fruit as a meal and already tasted it in her mind. When you start looking at other men and thinking of them, believe me, you are already halfway to adultery. That tree wasn't intended for food or for meeting the needs of man. That's why Eve didn't have to look at it and think of its attractiveness. Every day you look at men, work and communicate with them, because they are everywhere. If you perceive them in the right way, their constant presence isn't a problem. But as soon as you begin to deliberately see that '*the tree is good for food, that it is pleasant to the eyes, and a tree desirable to make one wise*', everything will go wrong, as in the case with the first people."

"Yes, Rita, you're right. I want to repent. I don't want everything to go wrong in my world. I have enough problems."

Vera had a bigger problem. Crying and eyes swollen with tears, she came to Rita and told her the story of her adultery. She did it deliberately to take revenge on her husband for her suffering, but that act had a completely opposite effect. She didn't feel better. She was disgusted with herself and eaten up with guilt. She couldn't look her husband in the eye and didn't know what to do. Her husband wouldn't forgive her. That was the only thing that he would never be able to forgive. How to keep living?"

"Dear Vera! You're not the first to get hooked. Let's read what the Word of God says:

> Then the scribes and Pharisees brought to Him a woman caught in adultery. And when they had set her in the midst, they said to Him, "Teacher, this woman was caught in adultery, in the very act. Now Moses, in the law, commanded us that such should be stoned. But what do You say?" This they said, testing Him, that they might have something of which to ac-

cuse Him. But Jesus stooped down and wrote on the ground with His finger, as though He didn't hear. So when they continued asking Him, He raised Himself up and said to them, "He who is without sin among you, let him throw a stone at her first." And again He stooped down and wrote on the ground. Then those who heard it, being convicted by their conscience, went out one by one, beginning with the oldest even to the last. And Jesus was left alone, and the woman standing in the midst. When Jesus had raised Himself up and saw no one but the woman, He said to her, "Woman, where are those accusers of yours? Has no one condemned you?" She said, "No one, Lord." And Jesus said to her, "Neither do I condemn you; go and sin no more."

                                 ∽ John 8:3–11

Jesus was the only one who had the right to condemn that woman, because He alone was without sin. But He didn't do that. He didn't condemn her, but forgave and showed mercy that she didn't deserve. His mercy and forgiveness gives the power to sin no more.

Look, here it's also written:

If we confess our sins, He is faithful and just to forgive us our sins and to cleanse us from all unrighteousness.   ∽ 1 John 1:9

You confessed your sin and God forgave you and cleansed you with His blood. Now just accept His forgiveness and move on, for God is loving and kind."

Then Alla came. She needed to talk right away. Alla repented for her thoughts, which were bombarding her.

When Rita and Alla prayed together, they realized that during that prayer, some wall, or kind of barrier, had fallen. They felt that something would happen soon. Indeed it did, after that repentance within the week her husband quitted taking narcotic pills. He had not taken heavy drugs for a long time, didn't drink or smoke, but couldn't give up taking painkillers with a strong effect. That was the last thing that kept him in the world of addictions.

Often, wives don't realize that they are some kind of obstacle on their husbands' way to liberation in the spiritual world.

The husband and the wife are one flesh; that is, they are united as one. And the best thing that the wife can do to help her husband is to become free as well.

Invisible chains keep them in bondage together.

We understand that the blind can't lead the blind, because both will fall into the pit.

Some wives experience physical agonies, never taking drugs. The spiritual world is real, and it can't be denied. Spouses are tied together by one chain, and to break the chain, the wife needs to take the path of freedom, because only by doing so, can she help her husband. Having become free, she can boldly win him back from the enemy."

CHAPTER 11

Fight Against the Enemy, but For Your Husband

"Hello girls! Well, everyone is present, so let's start the group. Let's begin with praise."

"I can't figure out how this singing can help me in solving my problems?" A new girl named Lyuda asked.

"Look, Lyuda! Do as you're told! Okay, you don't understand, but why are you bringing everybody down?" Lorena snapped.

"I'm not! I just want to understand how I will be helped by what we are doing here. If I wanted to sing, I would take vocals lessons or, in extreme cases, could sing at the table after drinking some alcohol to get relaxed, so to speak." Lyuda retorted.

"Listen, you remind me of me, when I started attending the group. I also couldn't get what was what. It was so unusual," Lorena said.

"Please, don't be mad at me. Maybe I asked rudely, but I really want to understand what is what." she answered.

"We aren't mad. It's just strange that, as you say, it's normal to sing after drinking some alcohol. When people dance in clubs and at concerts, raise their hands and throw flowers at the feet of their idols, that's normal, but when it comes to singing and opening our hearts before God and raising our hands to him, people don't understand." Lorena answered.

"All right, girls. Is there someone else who doesn't understand why we praise God?" Rita interrupted the conversation.

"Yes, there is! I also don't understand." another exclaimed.

"Okay, let's briefly talk about this. Lorena, could you tell us please? said Rita.

"Sure, I'll tell you, but please feel free to add something, if anything.

Praise

The Bible says that we should praise the Lord on all kinds of instruments. God lives among the praises of His people. God loves when He is praised, because He alone is worthy of praise. In Heaven, angels constantly sing praise to Him, and when we are in Heaven, we believers, will also praise and worship Him.

Praise is one of the weapons of our warfare. The devil is defeated when we sing to God and praise Him. The devil has no choice but to run away, because he can't do anything to people who praise and worship God.

When we raise our hands, we declare victory. When Moses raised his hands, the army of Israel won. That's why we also need to raise our hands.

Let me tell you the testimony of one businessman.

The daughter of a famous businessman got into an accident, after which she had psychiatric problems. She was placed in a psychiatric hospital. She didn't recognize her father. People were praying for her for about seven years, but nothing changed. Then God spoke to the heart of her father that he had to praise Him. At first, he resisted, because he couldn't understand what to praise for. But after a while, he surrendered and began to praise and worship God. On the same day, when he came to his daughter, she fell into his arms and was completely healed. Wherever God is praised, huge miracles happen and radical solutions come.

When I don't know what to do, and when life pushes me into a deadlock, I start to passionately praise God and worship Him for His wonderful deeds. And never once did He remain indifferent."

"Now it's clear to me. Let's praise the Lord," Lyuda said.

After praising God, the girls continued on with the group. This time they tried to understand how and with whom they needed to fight.

> For though we walk in the flesh, we do not war according to the flesh. For the weapons of our warfare are not carnal but mighty in God for pulling down strongholds, casting down arguments and every high thing that exalts itself against the knowledge of God, bringing every thought into captivity to the obedience of Christ... ∽ 2 Corinthians 10:3–5

God has given us everything needed for victory. But sometimes, instead of attacking a real enemy, we fight against innocent victims. Therefore, it is important for us to understand who our enemy is, so that we can defeat him.

"Girls, remember how we talked about anger. I told you how I nearly murdered my husband, and you shared your reactions. It was because we didn't understand that our husbands aren't our enemies. It seemed to us that they got what they deserved. It is important to understand who is behind all this horror, who the author is of any addiction and who our enemy is. Our enemy is the devil who tries to destroy our husbands through drugs or alcohol. Our husband is a victim of our common enemy. He is enslaved by Satan and needs to be set free. It is necessary to learn to separate a person from their actions. Man is beautiful, being created in the image and according to the likeness of God. But his actions can be terrible. God separates man from sin. Man sins because he lives in error and doesn't know the truth.

Remember we read the story of the demon-possessed man? When Jesus released him from demonic possession, he became a different person. Before he did awful things, but after the demons went out, he became wonderful, well-groomed and well-dressed, and felt the leading to serve God and to preach the gospel. The reason for his terrible behavior was the demons which controlled his life.

If you were going somewhere and some bird flew over you and dropped a so to say, "little, dirty greeting" on you, you wouldn't say that you had become what that bird left for you. If a person had a septic wound, he or she wouldn't become the wound, and if a person had a cancerous tumor, the person wouldn't become the cancer. Any splinter or dirt doesn't become a part of a person, but prevents them from living a life of freedom; it hurts, spoils the appearance etc. Sin is not a part of a person and it can be washed away. The blood of Jesus washes away all sin. Therefore, you don't need to call your husband a drug addict or an alcoholic. These are just splinters under the names 'drug addiction' and 'alcoholism'.

When we separate a person from their actions, we will be able to fight for them and against sin, defeating the enemy.

The doctor separates a person from a disease and treats the disease. God doesn't treat us based on our actions. It doesn't mean that if we do the wrong things, God doesn't love us, but if we are good, He loves us again. Or if you serve Him, He treats you well, but if you don't serve, His attitude towards you is bad. No, God's heart is not like that.

He loved us when we were still sinners, and gave His life for sinners.

Thus, Jesus separated sin from man.

He takes away the sin that's in you, and you become pure and sinless. He doesn't evaluate you based on your sins. He helps you to change. This is the heart of God.

So stop fighting with your husband, but step out against the real enemy. Fight for your husband and arrest him from the captivity of the enemy. God will help you in this battle, because He is on your side.

One of the strongest weapons God gave us is prayer and fasting. If you believe and pray, God will answer your prayers. Just ask God with all your heart. Pray together with someone and pray for each other. When we pray for someone, it's easy for us to believe that God will answer. Two can pray better that one. When one gets tired, the other will support him. It is easier to overcome difficulties together, because there is great power in unity. Ask God for His protection and defense. Ask Him to keep your husband in all his ways. Ask for mercy and grace. Ask for repentance and freedom. Ask a lot.

In prayer, we can fight. God gave us power. And in prayer we need to apply this power. Develop your prayer life.

Fight in prayer. You have the power to bind the addiction and command it to go away.

In this case, it makes no sense to fight with consequences. You need to hit the root of the problem.

It happens that the main problem is not drug addiction, but rejection. A person becomes a drug addict because they want to be accepted by people. When you sincerely pray for your husband, God will certainly reveal how you should pray and what you should fight against.

Make friends with the Holy Spirit. He will teach you how to pray and will lead you in prayer. And He is always ready to listen to you.

THE HOLY SPIRIT is the most attentive and perceptive listener.

Don't think that if God already knows all your feelings and problems, you don't need to tell Him about them.

Most likely, since childhood you have gotten used to the fact that nobody was serious about your desires and feelings. But understand that the Holy Spirit isn't like that. He cares about everything that's important to you and that's inside of you.

You have the right to feel pain when you are hurt, and you have the right to be angry, displeased, and the like.

Often people who behave disorderly, like those who get drunk or take drugs, demand that we don't express our feelings about that and pretend that nothing has happened.

But it's not true. It has really happened. Of course, you can't be happy about it. You have the right to be dissatisfied.

Begin to talk with Him today and tell Him about everything. Tell Him for example, this way:

'Holy Spirit, I invite You to communicate with me. I want to tell You about how in my childhood I was hurt when my cat got sick. I cried, I felt so sorry for it. I didn't want it to die. I was afraid of losing a friend. And my mother scoffed at me, saying, 'Well, what are you roaring about? It's no big deal. The cat is dying.' Therefore when it died, I tried to not cry because I knew that my parents would laugh at me. I waited for the night time to cry so that no one would see me.

Holy Spirit, and now, when my husband comes home in a state of intoxication, I try to not cry, because he also mocks me and says that I consider myself to be Mother Teresa. And it hurts.'

When you are telling all this to God, believe me, don't blame your relatives or throw mud at them, but just talk about your feelings. The Holy Spirit knows everything, and He knows that your parents behaved in that way so as not to hurt you, but to protect you from pain, to try to diminish the significance of the illness or the death of the cat.

Your husband behaves in such a way because he simply can't cope with himself and his addiction. And due to his powerlessness, he wants you to solve the problem and to not consider it to be important. When you start telling God everything, He will take away the pain, step by step, word by word. In the process of communication, He will remind you of different events and instances of your life, and you can just tell Him everything as it is. Tell Him what you were afraid to say out loud even to yourself. And remember, for Him, your feelings are important, both those from your childhood and those that you have now."

It's important to see

Rita continued, **"Try to set far-reaching goals.**

Usually, people who are addicted don't make plans for the future. Their plans are made for a day or two at the most. In addition to that, all their plans are gradually reduced to getting their necessary drug.

If you manage to help your husband to see his future, this will be a big victory.

Don't forget that you need to see him successful and healthy. What you can see will happen in your life.

It is difficult to see a successful life when you come home and there is no furniture, but only a mess, and a husband who is just playing around.

But you need to see the situation differently, envision a new you, a restored relationship. The better you can see, the better the future will be ahead.

One day God told Abraham to look around him. All that he could see God promised to give him. If you learn to see, God will give you everything.

God led Abraham outside and showed him the stars, saying that Abraham would have so many descendants.

He showed Abraham the sand and said that just as one couldn't count the number of grains of sand, it would be impossible to count his descendants. At that time, Abraham didn't even have one descendant. Sarah was barren, and they were too old to have children. Everything around them spoke of not being able to change their life, but they didn't believe it. Try to envision change.

A mother saw her son preaching on a platform at a time when he didn't even go to church and didn't want to hear anything about a rehab center. He was a drug addict, but she pictured him to be completely different. After many years, her son stood on stage with a microphone, and she cried with happiness.

One wife saw her husband become a businessman driving an expensive car; not a drug addict lying in bed. After some time, he became a successful businessman.

Your vision of the future determines what will be in your life!"

C H A P T E R   1 2

The Name of Jesus

"**G**irls, Rita is unwell and asked me to teach the class today," Vera said. "I want to tell you about my victory. For a long time I couldn't talk about it. I wasn't sure, because I didn't know whether you would understand me, and it was just never the right time. Remember, last time we talked about how to fight and what kind of weapons God gave us? I want to tell my testimony about this.

Thank God my husband is already free from addiction, but I had to go through a lot of things while we were dealing with this problem.

My husband hadn't come to himself for several days. He had some kind of insanity. He saw hallucinations and his eyes were wild. Even if you didn't understand much, you would probably be able to recognize that look. You don't need to be a psychotherapist to do this. It's immediately clear. What he was saying was strange, incomprehensible and, frankly, very scary.

A few ambulances came to us and the paramedics tried to persuade us to place him in a psychiatric hospital, but we refused.

When we were having an appointment with a psychotherapist, I barely survived his strange behavior. He was tearing his jacket, twisting his arms and saying something incomprehensible. Every second I had to be near him. He was prescribed some psychotropic medicines, but they didn't help. After two days of taking them, he had a terrible attack.

His mother was with him and decided to see how he was sleeping. But he wasn't asleep, but was breathing heavily. His movements were constrained. His mother and father turned him on his back and tried to wake him up, but his eyes rolled up and he didn't hear them. His parents called an ambulance, but, as ill luck would have it, they had a long drive.

I got a call at work, so I excused myself and left so no one could guess that I had any problems, and I immediately rushed home.

When the doors of the elevator opened, I saw my mother-in-law standing on the landing with the phone. She was pale as she once again called the ambulance which had not arrived yet. There were also some neighbors with her.

I flew into the apartment. His father stood over him, shaking him and trying to unbend his legs and arms which were just like stone. He couldn't move even an inch. His father's face was red, probably, due to being nervous and his having high blood pressure.

I threw my things down and ran to the bed. His father walked away, clearing the way for me. I saw that the color of my husband's face was green and white, his tongue sank and his eyes were rolled up. He didn't hear or react to anything.

It became clear that there were only a few minutes left before he might pass away. In despair, I began to yell to God in such a way that the whole house could hear. I started shouting, 'He shall call upon Me, and I will answer him!' That was the first thing which came to my mind. Then I turned to my husband and said, 'Call upon Jesus!' I told him to repeat the name of Jesus. Jesus was the only word he heard and reacted to. He barely moved his tongue, but it was clear to me that he was saying 'Jesus.' As soon as he managed to repeat the name JESUS, he immediately came to himself. His feet and hands were no longer stone. He looked normal. And after three minutes, he was absolutely okay. He said that he had seen a vision and didn't hear us, and all that he heard was the name of JESUS. And when He repeated that name, everything around turned red. We realized that that was the action of the BLOOD OF CHRIST. He came to himself.

After another two minutes, the long-awaited ambulance finally arrived.

We told them about my husband's symptoms and the medicines he had taken. The paramedics took his blood pressure, examined him and said that he was fine. They looked at us with disbelief and said that it was impossible to get out of that condition and that he could not have woken himself up.

> If we this day are judged for a good deed done to a helpless man, by what means **he has been made well**, let it be known to you all, and to all the people of Israel, **that by the name of Jesus Christ of Nazareth**, whom you crucified, whom God raised from the dead, by Him this man stands here before you whole. This is the 'stone which was rejected by you builders, which has become the chief cornerstone.' **Nor**

**is there salvation in any other, for there is
no other name under heaven given among
men by which we must be saved."**

         ෨ Acts 4:9–12

Now I know that the name of Jesus is stronger than anything in the world, that God hears us, and that there are no desperate situations for Him. In any situation, call upon Jesus. He hears and answers. He doesn't want anyone to perish.

> Therefore God also has highly exalted Him and **given Him the name which is above every name**, that at the name of Jesus every knee should bow, of those in heaven, and of those on earth, and of those under the earth, and that every tongue should confess that Jesus Christ is Lord, to the glory of God the Father.
>
>   ෨ Philippians 2:9–11

At the name of Jesus everything has to bow: every disease, danger or addiction. Absolutely everything must bow to the name of Jesus. There is nothing that can resist the name of the Lord Jesus Christ. His name is above every name, above every disease or problem. Absolutely everything is in His power.

Once I was in court, because one of my friends was tried. After all the hearings, the judge stood up and said:

'In the name of Ukraine, he is not guilty, and I order to release him from custody in the courtroom.'

My friend was immediately released. The judge didn't even think that his decision wouldn't be implemented. If he said to release someone in the name of

Ukraine, that person would be released. Perhaps the guards didn't agree with the judge's decision, but it didn't mean that they could refuse to obey.

The judge said so, because he had the authority given by the state of Ukraine. The entire system of justice had to obey the established authority.

So it is in the spiritual world. Jesus gave us the power of His name, and we say, 'In the name of Jesus, be free,' and don't have to doubt that demons and diseases will obey us.

The name of Jesus is above every name, above the name of Ukraine, above the name of any addiction or disease. The name of Ukraine or any other state, no matter how powerful it is, is powerless against demons, diseases and problems. But everyone and everything bows at the name of Jesus, because this name has power both in heaven and on earth. And Jesus gave us believers the power of His name, so that we can do His works on the earth.

But it is important for us to have a relationship with God and communicate with Him. Because there were people without knowing Jesus, who tried to use His name against demons. The demons beat them up and drove them away. When we pray in the name of Jesus, we don't speak magic words. We have to understand that Jesus is the Lord, the King, and everything is subject to Him. We need to communicate personally with Him.

Therefore, Jesus said that we should ask in the name of Jesus, and God will answer."

CHAPTER 13

Go All the Way

A year passed and the girls gathered to celebrate a special date.

For that year, all those who were persistent achieved excellent results. Almost all husbands had become free. Some husbands were in rehabilitation centers. Others were released without being sent to rehab centers. But most importantly, the girls changed and that was their greatest victory. There was still a lot to go through, but the main thing was that every one of them found God and followed Him.

"Girls, you know, lately I've been thinking about why people face the same situations but have different results. I've found some answers and want to share them with you today. There are difficult situations, serious problems and even tragedies in life. Some women have lost children, some suffer all their lives, never recovering from grief and thinking that their lives have come to an end, while others, being healed, start large ministries and help other people. Some can't find themselves after a divorce, while others start to live again. Some start to drink after being fired, while others start successful corporations. There are wives who are depressed about their husbands' addictions and remain in that state, but there are wives who recover despite all odds. There are girls who like you, have started attending the fellowship group, but now are sitting in the kitchen, smoking and thinking that I'm wrong, and don't love and understand them, and there are those of you who are here today because your lives have been changed.

You can talk a lot about the factors and reasons why some people do this and others do that, but I want to talk about **a very important thing. I think it will be useful.** To begin with, we will read the story from the Bible, the Book of Ruth.

Orpah and Ruth are two heroines, who survived after their husbands' deaths, who were sons of the same woman, their mother-in-law. Both of them had lost their husbands and both of them were not Jews. They had no protection, work and food. Their father-in-law had also died. But they wanted to go with their mother-in-law to Israel and set off on the road, although both of them had reasons to stay. But halfway to Israel, Orpah decided to go back. God had a purpose for her and an answer which was in the land of Israel. So He had an answer for Ruth. Ruth reached her destination, while Orpah didn't. Orpah began her journey in the same way as Ruth, and sincerely wanted to go, but when they were halfway through, she doubted and under the influence of persuasion, left all and returned to her land, to the home of her parents, where everything was customary.

Coming to God with our problems, we start on our way and believe that we will reach our destiny, overcome addictions and be able to make it work. But there will always be people and situations proving that this is futile, that there are no former drug addicts, that there is no guarantee, that we are simply wasting our time and life by going this way.

So Orpah wanted to go and she knew in her heart that it was right. She got rid of the first doubts, dealt with the attacks and went on, even with tears in her eyes. But 'sound' common sense and logic prevailed over faith and the prospect already seemed dubious. When we choose to follow God, this path doesn't seem easy at all, but this is the right path, because this is the only way to win. And with tears, Orpah didn't reach the goal and turned back. How sad it is to experience so much grief, to start the journey and to not reach the destination. How sad it is to make a decision and then cancel it.

Some people would say, 'I tried, but it didn't work. I went to church, I attended groups, I prayed and fasted, but I'm going to return to my old life, because I don't see any prospects and changes.'

Such women simply don't reach their goal, turning around halfway to their destiny and then giving up. It is always painful for me to see wives who have come so far to only then turn around halfway through, returning to their former chaos, simply because the path was hard and unknown and the chaos is easy and clear. The unknown frightens, because we don't know whether it will work or not. Don't be afraid! If you sincerely follow God, it will work! For God there is nothing impossible.

Ruth also didn't see what God had prepared for her. But what was the difference between these two women?

> But Ruth said: "Entreat me not to leave you, or
> to turn back from following after you; for wher-
> ever you go, I will go; and wherever you lodge,
> I will lodge; your people shall be my people,

and your God, my God. Where you die, I will die, and there will I be buried. The Lord does so to me, and more also, if anything but death parts you and me."

When she saw that **she was determined to go** with her, she stopped speaking to her.

Ↄ Ruth 1:16–18

She was determined

When a person is determined, people and circumstances can't stop them. Ruth was determined to follow God and had no hesitation. To understand whether a person will receive freedom or not, it is necessary to see if they are really determined to reach the goal. It will cost a lot, but if you are determined, you will get there. God told Joshua to be strong and of good courage. A firm decision determines whether we achieve the goal or not.

> But let him ask in faith, with no doubting, for he who doubts is like a wave of the sea driven and tossed by the wind. For let not that man suppose that he will receive anything from the Lord...

Ↄ James 1:6–7

Don't doubt! Doubting doesn't work.

Don't look back. If you've started to fight, go all the way.

> But Jesus said to him, "No one, having put his hand to the plow, and looking back, is fit for the kingdom of God."

Ↄ Luke 9:62

Do you remember the story of Lot's wife? The Lord decided to save Lot's family and began to take them out, but his wife, at some point decided to look back and became a pillar of salt. In that story God reveals to us the truth that we will definitely want to look back, because we haven't yet reached the place where we are going to. In our past life everything was known and familiar, although there were abominations, sins, scandals and drugs. Don't be deceived by the desire to look back.

And the same thing happened to God's people in the desert. They went a part of the way and suddenly began to recall their past life and looked back. That behavior postponed their entry into the Promised Land, where milk and honey flowed, for forty years.

God reveals to us the principles of victory, warning us that there will be a desire to give up everything and go back. There will be a desire to not keep walking, but it is necessary to go all the way, because only by doing so can you conquer the addiction.

People tend to get tired, feel bad and lose enthusiasm. It often happens that we start doing something with great faith in the success of it, but if we don't see significant changes after a while, we lose faith and get disappointed.

You can't consider the following thought to be making the decision to win: 'If during two months nothing changes and he doesn't stop acting like this and doesn't quit drugs, I will divorce him.' This is not a decision, when you are already looking at other men and imagining life with a different husband. It's not solving the problem when you think about how to introduce a new father to your son and how it will be.

In the Bible, the relationship between husband and wife is considered more important than the relationship between a mother and her son.

> Therefore a man shall leave his father and mother and be joined to his wife, and they shall become one flesh.　　　ൕ Genesis 2:24

Usually the world is different. It is believed that a mother under no circumstances would abandon an addicted son, but a wife is always able to divorce her addicted husband and build her life in a new way. God has different priorities. He looks at you and your husband as one. Each of you is a person but your marriage is indivisible. Let your thinking be the same as the thinking of God.

God loves persistence and rewards those people who don't have a 'plan B'.

Don't hesitate and don't look back! **Be determined and go all the way**.

No matter how deadlocked and unbearable the situation is, there is always a way out. In fact, there are two ways. Two robbers were hanging on the cross near Jesus. They were in the same situation. Both of them were sentenced to death, but one of them went to hell and the other went to the Kingdom of God. Make a firm decision to reach the goal, to withstand and overcome everything.

God is faithful. He doesn't reject those who come to Him, but helps them. It is important that no matter what, we follow Him. He is the most important in our lives. Without Him nothing will make sense: not business or work, family or children. The long-awaited freedom will turn into slavery, if there is no God in your life.

Remember, God brought His people out of slavery so that His people would serve Him and commune with Him. No matter how hard it is, always hold on to God. He is faithful. He won't betray. He is loving, kind and good. And you are His daughter, whom He will protect and bless.

Dear Alla, can you tell your story please?"

"Of course, with pleasure. It's been almost six months and I've been given the floor again." Alla replied with a smile.

"Although, what to tell? I'm just going to testify that my husband is free and we are serving the Lord together! And I managed to really forgive my dad. He repented and accepted Jesus as his Lord. God has changed my whole life. He has comforted and restored me, and now He leads me on. And this is what I wish to you all."

CHAPTER 14

He is Free,
But Why Am I Not Happy?

When starting to fight against the problem of their husband's addiction, I often hear from the following from wives, "If only he didn't drink! If only he didn't take drugs! And nothing else matters! I would demand nothing more from him, nothing from his job or anything else."

But this is only partly true, and to be quite honest, it's not really true at all.

As soon as your spouse is set free from drugs or alcohol, you immediately put forth 50 more new requirements: about the order in the house, any matters related to your children, problems with his job, and so on.

And the way you have communicated with your husband won't change unless you change yourself.

In addition, I wish to tell you one thing. If you don't change the way you talk to your husband, you risk losing your family.

Don't feel guilty

When a man is addicted, he constantly feels guilty, and therefore is often ready to suffer any punishment: screaming, scandals, control over his life and even the domination of his wife in the family. He agrees with her decisions only because he feels guilty towards her.

When the husband breaks free from addiction, he no longer feels guilty, and his wife can't manipulate him.

Before it was so comfortable! After her husband stopped getting drunk and caught with drugs, everything started to change over a few days' time. Her husband started giving her presents, helping with household, going shopping and doing anything to make it up to his wife because his guilt was eating him up inside.

He could now buy for his wife something that he wasn't allowed to buy for himself before, or go somewhere where he couldn't. Thus, her husband voluntarily loses his superiority and the wife starts to twist him around her finger. This is her way to avenge that pain that she has recently felt. But to be honest, she is no longer satisfied with this.

This revenge is a blow to the male ego, when a man must obey his wife and do what he doesn't want to do, or to do it not for love and pleasure, but because of a vile feeling of guilt.

But as he begins to rise up, he won't tolerate all this anymore. And then his wife starts to resent him and remembers the long haul she just went through and how many times she had forgiven him, making things worse and worse.

He begins to strive for a new life, but you want him to return to the old one.

At this point, one of two things happens: either he starts to drink (or take drugs) again, or you split up. I think it's stupid to go so far and finally to start back at the bottom of the ladder.

You need to trust again

When a person has been deceiving you for a long time, it's hard to not keep your head on a swivel all the time. But you need to start trusting again. You don't need to control his every step, you don't need to call him every 15 minutes and listen carefully to what's going on and where he is. Trust God Who is in him. This distrust and control upset a person and make them angry. It is very unpleasant when your loved one doesn't trust you and doesn't believe in you.

If he slips up, it's not the end

Sometimes after becoming free, a person gets into a trouble again. But think about a child who learns how to walk: he takes a step and falls down. Don't throw tantrums because of the fall. Just help him get up and take a few steps. Soon he will learn how to walk.

It is also important to not hide what has happened from your mentors. Sometimes wives don't want to reveal that their husbands are in trouble again, but that's wrong. This cover-up doesn't lead to anything good. "If I don't say anything, it's okay, because it's the last time he will do it," the wives think. This is a mistake because you need to speak up so the problem won't come back again.

Help him rise up

His success is your success. After all, you are a family. Don't be jealous of his success and don't compete with him. The family is not a competition between each other, but a team. When he was addicted, you were his savior and the breadwinner in the family. In fact, the burden of responsibility was on you, and everyone felt sorry for you. But now you are no longer the center of attention, and it might be difficult. Now nobody has sympathy for you, and sometimes they are even jealous of you.

Let him be the head of the family. Perhaps he won't be good right away and will make many mistakes. But this is normal because he has just dealt with the problem and is making his first steps at taking responsibility for the family. But I promise you that after a while, if you don't interfere, you will see that he can take care of the family like a fish in the water, and that you'd never be able to do it as well as he can. Men are able to make the right decisions and be responsible. Don't deprive him of this ability.

It is necessary to respect

What your husband needs is respect. It is very difficult to start respecting him after all that he's done. But respect is necessary for him to be able to achieve success. Moreover, it is hard to obey if you don't respect him. After all, his success is your success.

Believe in him. Don't humiliate or disrespect him.

Of course when he was addicted, you were used to making all of the decisions independently. You were used to the fact that everything depended on you. Perhaps, for the first time, your husband will 'play' the head of the family, but you just have to wait, and everything will fall into place. Because for so long he didn't take responsibility, it might be difficult for him to find the right balance between giving wise counsel and the directing the family. Therefore, he may still be aggressive for a while.

He needs to find himself, establish himself as the head of the family and begin to realize his potential. Don't interfere with this process.

A woman's happiness can be complete only if everyone in the family bears the responsibility intended for them by God. The husband is the head of the family. The wife is his helpmate. Everyone has different responsibilities in the family.

Jealousy over ministry

When the long-awaited freedom comes and your husband begins to live in a new way, his wife may feel jealous. She thinks, "He doesn't need any mentors! I will take care of him!" This is jealousy and control over his life. Believe me, the work is not over yet! So don't stop. Trust your mentors and allow your husband to develop.

He doesn't spend time with the family, as desired. He is always busy with ministry. One day he is talking on the phone a lot, another day he is looking for people like himself to help them. He works, he tries. He seems to be trying to catch up with what he has lost before; to catch up with everything but your relationship. And among all these wonderful and kind deeds, you don't understand where your place is, or your children's and family's. Don't judge him so strictly.

His behavior is like emerging from the water. If a person is under the water for a while, holding their breath, then after coming up for air, they start to quickly gasp for breath, gulp by gulp. He doesn't have time for intimate talk, he just wants to breathe. Give him time and pray to the Lord. God brought him out of the addiction, and in the same way He will help him find balance in everything.

Don't let past, unhealed pain steal your blessings

Read the story written in the book of 2 Samuel, chapter 6.

Michal, David's wife, despised David in her heart when he was leaping and twirling before the Lord. He was returning with victory from war and dancing in such a way that his underwear was visible. That's why Michal despised him and even said that he behaved shamelessly like one of the base fellows.

She said that because of her unhealed pain of rejection. Some time ago David had to leave her with her father, and for many years she was living without her husband. David couldn't take her with him because her father, King Saul, was hunting him down. She couldn't get free from that feeling of rejection. But freedom from those feelings was necessary for a happy life.

Snide remarks and arrogance won't bring happiness to the family.

When addicted, your husband was "absent". During that time, you may have had bitter feelings toward him, but you need to forgive him and get free from bitterness.

Due to such dishonor and condemnation, God restrained Michal from bearing children. She couldn't have children. God doesn't keep score in the family. God wants our hearts to be pure.

Even if, in the wife's opinion, her husband acts indecently or unworthily, God doesn't welcome judgment.

Especially when a person dances before their God, who gave them victory. May your husband be free to enjoy his victories, to sing and dance, and you need to share this joy with him.

Don't do what your husband should do

Having suffered a trauma, one girl fell into depression and never came down from the second floor of the house. Her mother brought her breakfast, lunch and dinner, and took care of her. But one day her mother died. On the second or third day, with pain and effort, the girl got out of bed for the first time in many years and went downstairs. Very often, when someone stops taking care of us, we have to learn to take care of ourselves.

Abraham Lincoln said, "You can't help people permanently by doing for them what they could and should do for themselves."

Let your husband be a complete person. A disabled person needs a constant care, but your husband is not disabled.

How to not return to the problem again

One boy fell out of his bed every night. Being bruised, he had to stand up and get back into bed. But one day he was tired of falling, and he decided to ask his father what to do so as not to fall.

His father answered him,"'Son, you just need to get deeper into your bed, and you won't fall."

It's very simple: Go deeper into God! May God's fire always burn in your heart!

Kary Rowen

Facebook
https://www.facebook.com/karyrowen

E-mail
karyrowen@gmail.com

www.ingramcontent.com/pod-product-compliance
Lightning Source LLC
Chambersburg PA
CBHW061538120726
48001CB00004B/1616